A New Life, A New Menu: An Almanac of Belonging

MARINA BARONAS

Dedication

To my grandmother, who sowed love into the earth and taught me that food is a language of devotion.

To my mother, whose quiet strength carried us through uncertainty and whose belief in me never wavered.

To my family—by birth, by bond, and by shared story—your presence has been the thread through every season.

To my tribe, those I've worked besides, broken bread with, laughed with, and leaned on—this book carries your fingerprints.

To my sons, who carry my story forward in their bones.

To those who serve—seen or unseen—may you never forget: you are not invisible here.

Copyright © 2025 Crafted By Soul LLC.

All rights reserved. No part of this book may be reproduced or used in any manner without the prior written permission of the copyright owner, except for the use of brief quotations in a book review.

First edition September 2025.

Edited by Cortni Merritt at SRD Editing Services
Cover art and Layout by Jonas Peres

This book is a memoir. It reflects the author's present recollections of experiences over time. Some names and characteristics have been changed, some events have been compressed, and some dialogue has been recreated. For privacy reasons, names, locations, and dates may have been changed.

No part of this publication may be reproduced, stored, or transmitted in any form or by any means, electronic, mechanical, photocopying, recording, scanning, or otherwise without written permission from the publisher. It is illegal to copy this book, post it to a website, or distribute it by any other means without permission.

Marina Baronas asserts the moral right to be identified as the author of this work.

Table of Contents

Dedication   5

Introduction: A Place at the Table   9

Chapter 1: Seeds of Passion   13

Chapter 2: Seasons of the Garden   21

Chapter 3: The Soul of Hospitality   29

Chapter 4: The Day of the Parade   35

Chapter 5: A Bond Beyond Borders   41

Chapter 6: The Great Leap   47

Chapter 7: The Journey Begins   55

Chapter 8: The First "Real" Day   69

Chapter 9: Reflections and Realities   75

Chapter 10: The Rhythm of Service   81

Chapter 11: Between Two Worlds   89

Chapter 12: Roots and Wings   93

Chapter 13: The Great Return   101

Chapter 14: Echoes of Understanding   105

Chapter 15: The Weight of Departure   113

Chapter 16: The Glances of Transition   119

Chapter 17: The Weight of Becoming	125
Chapter 18: The Quiet Fires of Progress	133
Chapter 19: Leading with Humanity, an Ongoing Journey	141
Chapter 20: The Beginning of Something Grand	147
Chapter 21: Unveiling the Dream	157
Chapter 22: Between Waves and Walls: A New Horizon	163
Chapter 23: The Vicious Cycle	169
Chapter 24: The Phantom of Fulfillment	173
Chapter 25: The Illusion of Stillness	177
Chapter 26: The Mirage of Success	191
Chapter 27: The Collapse of Certainty	199
Chapter 28: The Shattered Path Forward	205
Chapter 29: The Core of My Becoming	211
Chapter 30: The Power of Self-Compassion	217
Chapter 31: Hospitality as a Way of Life—Purpose	223
Chapter 32: Embracing Joy and Presence in the Everyday	227
Chapter 33: Final Reflections: The Legacy of Hospitality	233
Acknowledgements	237
Author Bio	239

INTRODUCTION

A Place at the Table

There are silences not born of peace but of trembling—moments when the soul holds its breath before the weight of the world shifts, when the stillness before service begins feels like a sacred hush. In those moments, there is no applause, no spotlight, no pressure. Only the quiet comprehension that something meaningful is about to unfold. I have spent the better part of my life listening to those silences in dining rooms, kitchens, offices, and hearts.

I was raised in Russia and came of age in a world where hospitality was not a job—it was a way of being. It was an instinct, passed down not in books or business plans but through the movements of women in the kitchen, through stories told over tea, through the way my grandmother, who lived in Lithuania, always made space for one more guest, no matter how little we had. Her table was never only a place to eat; it was a sanctuary. A place where hunger, sorrow, joy, and memory sat down together. That table is where I first learned that to feed someone is to love them and that dignity can live even in the smallest acts.

I did not know then that hospitality would become my life's work, but looking back, I understand it was always with me.

I came to the United States after college, graduating class of 2002, carrying a degree in hospitality and a minor in psychology, but more than that, I carried hunger. Not just for opportunity but for understanding. I wanted to know people. Systems. Cultures. Pain. I wanted to see how food and service bridged what language sometimes couldn't. Over twenty-seven years, I worked my way through nearly every layer of this world: server, manager, leader, operator, mother, mentor. I cried in walk-ins and laughed over closing drinks. I broke, rebuilt, grew. Sometimes I led well. Sometimes I didn't. But I never stopped caring.

This, I believe, is what defines us in hospitality: the refusal to become indifferent. To show up with heart, even when it's hard. Especially when it's hard.

This book was not written from the top of the mountain. It was written from the road. It is not a polished guide to leadership or a manual for success. It is an almanac—seasonal, lived, messy, true. It is the story of a life shaped across borders—born in Germany, raised between Russia, Azerbaijan, and Lithuania—where hospitality wasn't taught, it was inherited. Inherited through hands that cooked without measuring, through doors that opened without question, through the quiet belief that how we care for one another is the truest measure of who we are. That spirit traveled with me to America at nineteen, tucked beside my degree and my hunger to understand more than systems—I wanted to understand people. This is not a story of mastery, but of becoming. Of learning to lead not through control but through care. Of choosing growth over perfection. Of discovering that leadership, like hospitality, begins with service—offered honestly and with integrity. It teaches you to care without condition, to hold space for others without losing yourself. Over time, that practice becomes who you are.

Hospitality, at its core, is about humanity. To work in this field is to practice your humanity over and over again, until it seeps into your bones. Until you cannot separate the profession from the person.

Throughout these pages, you'll encounter stories from both the front lines and behind the scenes—spanning everything from humble mom-and-pop eateries to the gilded spaces of luxury hotel chains, where creating unforgettable experiences is not a goal but a standard. You'll feel the weight of unspoken rules, the joy of connection, the pain of burnout, the beauty of redemption. You'll meet the mentors who changed me, mistakes that shaped me, and moments of grace that kept me going.

You'll also hear my voice—a voice forged between cultures, between worlds, between the past and the future. It is a voice that still believes, stubbornly and fiercely, that there is nobility in service. That there is wisdom in tradition and courage in change. That food is a language and hospitality is a kind of faith.

I wrote this book for anyone who has ever felt invisible while giving everything. For those who wonder if they are allowed to rest, to evolve, to lead with heart in a world that often demands detachment. For the young ones, at the beginning, unsure whether this world will hold them, and for the seasoned veterans, whose hands have carried the weight of generations.

I want to say: there is space for you here. This life is not easy, but it is abundant. It will test you. It will teach you. It will open parts of you that you did not know existed.

As I write later in this book:

"Leadership is not a destination—it is a state of being. To lead is to be willing to break your own heart a little each day in service of something greater. It is to choose compassion over control, learning over knowing, and humility over certainty."

This book is a mirror, a letter, a meal. A reflection of a life lived in pursuit of something sacred. I hope, in these pages, you find pieces of yourself—not simply as a professional but as a human being seeking connection, meaning, and a place to belong.

So, please—sit. Breathe. There is a place for you at this table.

Let us begin.

CHAPTER 1

Seeds of Passion

The air was thick with the mesmeric fragrance of roses, peonies, petunias, and gladioluses, their colors spilling over the edges of the garden beds like a spectrum of pigments danced into existence, transforming the landscape into a vivid masterpiece. I was six years old, sitting on a small wooden stool by the open kitchen window at my grandmother's *dacha*, a summer home nestled outside Vilnius. A melodic reverberation of bees pollinating the blossoms intermingled with the faint clattering of jars and the gentle gurgling of strawberries cooking on the stove. It was one of those rare mornings when everything felt suspended beyond time's reach, as though the world outside could wait. There was a stillness in the air—an ethereal serenity that invited me to pause, to breathe, to simply exist in the moment.

From my perch, I saw the rows of fruit trees—apple, pear, cherry, and plum—standing tall and proud, their limbs bent under the heavy load of ripening fruit. Beyond them, the black and red currant bushes formed a tangled border, their jewel-like berries gleaming under the early summer sun. The greenhouse stood at the edge of the garden, its glass windows fogged with humidity, cocooning tomatoes, cucumbers, peppers, and other treasures nurtured by my grandmother's attentive hands. Closer to the house grew rows of strawberries, their rubies peeking out from beneath the green leaves, and the raspberry bushes, already heavy with sweet berries. This was her world—a realm she had cultivated with care, patience, and near-sacred devotion to the soil, each plant a reflection of the silent, endless assiduity she gave to the earth.

Inside the kitchen, the air vortexed with steam and sweetness. My grandmother—her hands lined with age, still possessing an unyielding dexterity—stood by the timeworn stove, stirring a pot of strawberries. She worked methodically, her every move a practiced ritual, as if each spoonful of jam she created carried a piece of her heart. The wooden spoon scraped gently against the bottom of the pot, releasing a burst of sugary aroma each time.

She smiled and called out to me, "Come over, *моя маленькая*," her voice warm and melodic, a comforting sound that melted the hardest of days.

I hopped off the stool and hurried to her side. She offered me a small spoon filled with the bubbling mixture. The heat of the jam tingled my tongue, but the taste—sweet, slightly tart, and vibrant—made me giggle with delight.

"What do you think?" she asked, her eyes flickering.

I nodded eagerly, and she laughed, a sound as comforting as the warmth of her kitchen.

***

Growing up in a military family meant constant change, and my father's assignments took us to different corners of the world. We moved from country to country, language to language. At home, we lived simply, eating the food that was allocated by the military—canned meat, rice, and potatoes. The lack of variety never bothered me; it was simply how things were. But every summer, like clockwork, I would spend my days at my grandmother's house. My brother typically stayed with my parents, but for me, the summers were a sacred time to immerse myself in the comforting lilt of my grandmother's home.

My grandmother's home became a sanctuary, a refuge where life slowed down enough to savor each moment. It was a constant place that shaped me into who I would become. My grandmother was more than my father's mother; she was a protector of our heritage, a teacher of life's most important lessons, and above all, a hostess who recalled all the stories of our family and taught me the meaning of hospitality.

The time spent with my grandmother was about preserving kinship. This was her essence—her tie to the earth, hands weaving together passion and care with every meal. The garden she tended so tirelessly reflected her soul: strong, resilient, and nurturing. Each plant was a part of her; each fruit, a product of years spent cultivating not only the land but also the innate essence of what it meant to be family. I was spoiled by her garden—strawberries, raspberries, currants—each burst of sweetness a reminder of the love she poured into the land and the fruits it gave in return. The land, the fruit, the food, and the love were intertwined, like a thread weaving our family together through every season.

Beyond the house stood the glass-enclosed gazebo where my grandmother and I retreated on rainy summer days. The metal roof sounded with the tempo of the rain, but inside, we were sheltered, playing card games and sipping mint-berry tea, laughing at the stories my grandmother shared, her voice mellow as she recounted fables of her youth in the Pskovskaya region.

"My grandma always spoiled me with carefully prepared traditional Russian dishes," she said. She spoke of the rich heritage of Russian cuisine she inherited.

I listened, spellbound by her stories, as the rain danced against the glass and the world outside disappeared. In those glimmers of time, I found peace—not only in the shelter of the gazebo but in the warmth of her presence, the gentleness in her voice, and the comfort of knowing her legacy of care would endure. When the rain finally ceased and we opened the gazebo door, the air was saturated with the freshness of the earth, renewed and clean.

"Babushka," I exclaimed. "Look outside!"

The sun peeked through, casting reflections on the raindrops gripping to the flower leaves, turning them into a living Monet painting. In these rare moments, when the world slowed down and my grandmother and I found ourselves in harmony with nature and each other, I found solace. It was as if time itself paused to honor the beauty of the earth and the togetherness we shared, wrapped in the intimacy of a cup of tea and the subdued serenity of the garden.

***

On sunny mornings, my grandmother and I baked together in her kitchen, filling the air with the intoxicating scent of fresh pastries. Poppy seed roulade, a dish with sentimental significance to me, was one of our favorites. The delicate dough was rolled with a decadent filling of poppy seeds, sugar, and butter, creating a perfect balance of sweetness and earthiness.

My grandmother's hands moved gracefully, folding the dough precisely, her voice soft as she explained the art of making the roulade—how to knead the dough with patience, how to let it rise enough before it was ready for the oven. I watched her, mesmerized by her expertise and the way she transformed simple ingredients into something extraordinary. The process of baking with her was a lesson in care, in taking the time to perfect something small yet meaningful.

As the roulade baked, the house filled with warmth and the tantalizing aromas of butter and sweet poppy seeds. We sat at the kitchen table, cutting slices of the roulade, and sipping freshly brewed tea. The first bite always felt like a taste of summer—comforting, sumptuous, and full of the adulation she infused into every meal.

"Так сладко и вкусно," ("So sweet and delicious"), I couldn't refrain from expressing. It was these moments—uncomplicated, yet transformative—that taught me the value of presence and the importance of creating space for the ones we love. The lessons of

compassion, patience, and attention to detail were not only in the food my grandmother prepared but in the way she lived her life, every day, with grace and care.

***

Flowers undeniably enchanted her. Roses of every shade bloomed in profusion, their velvety petals ranging from deep crimson to soft pink, while her favorite peonies with their fluffy blooms swayed gently in the summer breeze. Gladioluses—tall and proud with vibrant spikes of color—added a touch of elegance to the landscape. Tulips and marigolds in her flower beds displayed a riot of color, their petals shining brightly against the verdant backdrop. Her garden was a tapestry of hues, a constant celebration of the seasons and the tender care she gave it. She spent hours walking through her garden, inhaling the scents of her flowers, and sometimes when she wasn't in a hurry, she'd pluck a blossom or two, tucking them into vases scattered throughout the house. For my grandmother, the garden was not only unambiguously a place of beauty—it was a way to reconnect with herself, to find solace in the small vignettes of nature's wonder.

As the summer days faded and the crispness of fall permeated the air, my grandmother began her serious preparations for the winter months. "*Marina, иди сюда и подай мне баночки пожалуйста,*" ("Marina, come here and give me the jars, please"), she would call for me. The basement, where she stored her canned goods, became a place of immense importance. The shelves were lined with jars of preserves—tomatoes, cucumbers, berries, pickled vegetables, and sweet jams, each jar sealed with care. She spent long afternoons in the basement, methodically filling jars with the summer's bounty, ensuring they lasted through the cold months. The cool stone walls of the basement were comforting, and the earthy smell that lingered in the air reminded me of the earth's eternal cycle—the promise that the land would rest but always return with the warmth of the next spring. The basement was her sanctuary, a place where the fruits of her labor were stored, preserved for future generations.

In these cadences, I saw how my grandmother viewed her relationship with the earth—every season was a lesson in patience and resilience, a deep understanding that nothing lasts forever, but with the right care, the cycles continue. She taught me that what we put into the soil, into our work, and into the hearts of others always returns to us in one form or another. It was not simply the harvest—it was the way we nurtured everything around us, the way we cared for the earth, the people, and the moments we were given. Her lessons on this were subtle, woven into the fabric of her daily life, and yet they stay with me forever.

Then, as the first frost touched the ground, the greenhouse was prepared for winter. The last of the tomatoes and cucumbers were picked, and the remaining plants were covered and sheltered from the harsh winter weather. It was a delicate balance, one my grandmother understood better than anyone—how to make the most of what the earth gave and how to prepare for the months when it rested. She had an unspoken wisdom of seasons, transitions, and the careful stewardship required to make it all come together. To her, winter wasn't a time of scarcity; it was a time to reflect, to rest, and to prepare for the next cycle. Even in the quiet, dormant months, her garden continued to nourish our spirits—through the preserves, the memories, and the anticipation of the next harvest.

**

Beyond the garden, there was more to my grandmother's nurturing spirit. In the mornings, we walked down the dirt road to the nearby farm to fetch fresh milk. We'd pass through fields, the whiff of dairy cattle hanging in the air, and make our way to the small barn where the cows stood, grazing lazily under the open sky. The farmer, a kind man with a weathered face and gentle hands, milked the cows, and we waited, taking in the peaceful surroundings. Afterward, we walked back to the dacha, carrying the milk in large glass jars.

Once home, we sat on the porch, surrounded by the lush fruit trees of my grandmother's garden, and drink the warm milk straight from the jar. I remember how the taste was a treat—fresh, rich, creamy, and full of life; it tasted like the innate essence of the earth. The sun filtered through the trees, casting dappled shadows across our faces, and we sipped quietly, savoring the simplicity of the moment. I can picture us, both with milk mustaches, giggling at some small joke, the world shrinking to the two of us and the sun-dappled porch. The milk, the warm breeze, and the lush green of the garden wrapped me in security and peace, a silent glee only my grandmother's presence offered.

At home, my grandmother got to work making meals that tasted like love itself—pierogies stuffed with potatoes or cherries, full-bodied soups, and hearty stews. I could always count on the delicious aroma of homemade dishes filling the house, warming the air with the promise of comfort. I recall the way she hummed softly as she worked, the rhythm of her hands creating a feast that brought people together around the table. Every meal she made was a reminder of the care she put into each bite. Whether it was a simple stew or an elaborate dish, each meal reflected her dedication to those she loved.

My grandmother also grew fresh mint and wild berries, which she used to make fragrant teas. I remember the gentle, soothing scent of mint leaves drying in the sun and how teas made from her garden warmed us on cool evenings. The tea, brewed with precisely the right amount of sweetness, was always more than a mere drink—it was a moment of connection, of unobtrusive companionship. Whether we were sitting at the kitchen table or watching the rain from the gazebo, the tea we shared remind me now that the simplest things often hold the deepest meaning.

***

As I grew older, I came to understand it wasn't simply the jam, the strawberries, or the tea that made those moments special—it was the way my grandmother wove love into everything she did. Agape grew and thrived in the garden, the kitchen, and the warmth of the sun-dappled porch. She gave me a revelatory awareness of the importance of nurturing—not only the earth but the relationships we hold dear. Her lessons were not always spoken, but they were woven into the intrinsic fabric of her actions. Through her, I learned that love is a garden, and if we tend to it with patience and care, it will bloom in ways we never imagined.

As I sit now, thinking of her—the way she nurtured everything she touched, from the soil to the people she loved—I carry her lessons with me. Her legacy lives on, not only in the flowers and fruits of the earth but also in the way I nurture those I love, exactly as she did. In the act of caring, I honor her. Her garden, her kitchen, her inconspicuous strength, and her unwavering benevolence for family—these are the gifts my grandmother passed on to me, and they are the gifts I carry with me as I continue to nurture my own life and family.

CHAPTER 2

Seasons of the Garden

I was born in 1980 in Rostock, Germany, yet my earliest memories are wrapped in the warmth and aridity of Azerbaijan, a land where the sun's intensity lingers long into the night and the earth seems to absorb every ounce of heat. At three, my family moved to Sangachaly, a village nestled fifty kilometers from Baku, and the world I encountered there—vast, barren, and unyielding—was far removed from the gentle temperate climates of my German birthplace. The landscapes felt endless, suffocating in their stillness. The sky stretched on in a pale, oppressive blue only broken by the occasional silhouette of a distant hill or a sparse tree. The air, heavy with dust, hung thick above the dry earth, and every window in our home appeared to rattle with the heat, as if even the house itself struggled to remain still.

In the middle of this unrelenting climate, I found a fleeting escape each summer, a time when I could leave behind the suffocating heat of Azerbaijan for the gentle embrace of Lithuania. It was with my grandmother—Babushka—that I found relief from the heaviness of the desert and from the loneliness of a place I could never quite understand. The transition from the sun-scorched plains of Azerbaijan to the verdant beauty of Lithuania felt like a journey into a completely different world. Babushka's dacha, nestled in the rolling hills of Vilnius, was a sanctuary—a refuge that represented a stark contrast to the arid expanses of Azerbaijan.

At the close of each school year, I was sent away—lifted from the dry heat of Azerbaijan and placed onto a plane bound for Vilnius, where my grandmother lived in a faded apartment not far from the city's old heart. Her rooms were spare yet deliberate—free of clutter and robust with presence. Damask rugs hung on the walls like heirlooms of silence, and each piece of furniture stood carefully appointed, not for comfort alone but for the quiet dignity it lent the space. From there, the days unfolded not in haste but in slow procession, governed by rituals and the subtle passing of light through gauze curtains.

Each week, we turned our backs to the city, traveling to the dacha—a small house nestled among whispering birches and the wild hush of grasses. It was there, amid the shifting moods of sky and soil, that summer took root in me.

It began with the familiar drone of the trolleybus, its old wooden floors creaking beneath the weight of weary passengers, the soft buzz of the overhead lights providing a gentle soundtrack as we passed through the elegant streets. As the urban landscape gave way to the outskirts, I felt the air begin to shift—the city's noise dissolving, replaced by the quiet murmur of nature. The trolleybus slowed as we approached the forested hills, and once we disembarked, we walked the last few miles to the dacha, our footsteps falling in chime with the earth's breath.

Babushka, ever strong and unhurried, carried bags laden with supplies, her movements so fluid and purposeful that it was impossible not to be caught up in the gentle grace with which she navigated the landscape. Even with the encumbrance of her load, she never seemed burdened. There was an assurance in her step, a connection to the land, which made everything she did seem effortless. Babushka's dacha, with its cool, clean air and fertile land, was a place where the load of the world felt like it fell away. The garden there was her pride—a living testament to her connection to the land, to tradition, and to the natural rhythms that governed life in Lithuania. The garden wasn't simply a place to grow food; it was a space where she tended to her thoughts, where she reconnected with her heritage in a way that felt deeply spiritual. Each season brought new lessons, not simply for farming but for life itself. I helped Babushka harvest the plums, apples, and berries from the trees, feeling the cool soil between my fingers as I worked. Every vegetable I pulled from the ground, every fruit I plucked from the trees, became an offering, a small gesture of care and gratitude for the earth. I learned early that nothing in this world came without patience.

The summers in Lithuania were an immersion in nature. Beyond the garden, there were the lakes, their clear waters providing relief from the summer heat. I spent hours swimming, my body weightless in the cool caress of the water, before venturing into the forests to gather wild berries. The motion of picking these berries felt like a small ritual, one that connected me to the earth and to Babushka in ways I didn't entirely understand at the time. The simple thrill of being outdoors, of tasting the wild sweetness of those berries was a reminder of the abundance that life had to offer when given the right care. Yet the most penetrating lessons I received from Babushka took place in the kitchen, where food became a language of its own. But her strength was not confined to quiet rituals. Long before I was born, she survived the war—a chapter she rarely spoke of but that lingered in her silences. Later, in a world that offered little space for women to lead, she rose to become director of finance at a television manufacturing company in Vilnius. It was a role few women held at the time, and fewer still while raising a child. She bore it all with quiet defiance—strong and soft in equal measure, like linen stretched over iron.

Babushka's cooking was a ritual—a form of storytelling passed down through generations. The kitchen was where we connected most deeply, not merely over the preparation of food but over shared glimpses of understanding and love. It was in this space I learned the true meaning of patience and perseverance. I remember well the summers when we would make *cepelinai*, traditional Lithuanian potato dumplings. It was an activity that invoked all my senses—the sharp scent of freshly peeled potatoes filling the kitchen, the warmth of the stove, and the texture of the meat mixture, carefully prepared by Babushka with ground pork, herbs, and a dash of onion or garlic.

Using my small, impatient hands to shape the dumplings and press the potato mixture around them felt like a trial. My first attempts were far from perfect, often too large or misshapen. But Babushka never once hurried me, never once told me I wasn't doing it right. Instead, she remained calm, teaching me the value of care, of doing something slowly and with intention. It was through her that I came to understand that cooking was an act of devotion and patience, not simply for the food but for the people who would eventually enjoy it.

Then, there were the *Sausainiai Grybukai*, the mushroom-shaped cookies that became our summer tradition. These little creations, dipped in chocolate and carefully glued together with sugar syrup, required patience and precision—two qualities that Babushka embodied perfectly. We spent hours rolling out dough, shaping the little mushrooms, laughing together as we worked. There was an inherent jubilee in the process, in the shared effort to create something beautiful and delicious. As the cookies baked, the kitchen filled with the aromas of chocolate and butter, which carried with them the promise of home.

In the evenings, when the air grew cooler and the sun dipped below the horizon, Babushka lit the fire in the dacha's fireplace. The crackling flames cast a glow over the room, and we sat together, sipping tea, savoring the fruits of our labor. Whether it was a slice of homemade Napoleon cake or a plate of freshly baked cookies, the food was always accompanied by a reserved, comforting conversation. Babushka's voice was steady and soothing, and in those moments, the world outside disappeared. Time slowed down. The bond between us and the shared delight of being together became the only things that mattered. These moments of connection were more than simply pleasant memories; they were the foundation of my understanding of love, memory, and tradition.

Though our family had long lived in the arid stillness of Azerbaijan, things shifted after my grandfather passed away. In 1987, my father arranged for our relocation to the Kaliningrad region, closer to his mother. It was a quiet change, born more from necessity than ambition. The move brought us nearer to Lithuania in distance, but the emotional and environmental comparison was striking.

As much as I cherished my time in Lithuania, the juxtaposition of these two worlds—the fertile, abundant landscapes of Lithuania and the barren, resource-deprived region of Kaliningrad—was never lost on me. When my family moved to the Kaliningrad region, the difference between the two places became even more apparent. Kaliningrad Oblast, once a proud Prussian region, had fallen under Soviet control, and its once-thriving agricultural systems had crumbled under the encumbrance of inefficiency.

The landscape was marked by abandoned farms and run-down factories, their decay a visible testament to the struggles of the Soviet era. While Lithuania thrived in ways Kaliningrad could only imagine, it was evident that the region was struggling. The Soviet mainland heavily supported Kaliningrad, and despite the land's ability to produce food, it frequently suffered neglect. The markets were sparse, with shelves that rarely held more than the basics. By comparison, Lithuania's fertile soil, bolstered by Soviet resources, yielded abundance. There, the markets were filled with fresh produce, meats, and cheeses—a bounty that seemed like luxury in the bleak environment of Kaliningrad.

I was left with an impression that I didn't quite understand at the time after experiencing these two radically different worlds— Kaliningrad's bare shelves and Lithuania's thriving marketplaces brimming with fresh vegetables. I gained an appreciation for the worth of each item and each carefully cooked dish. In Lithuania, the ease of abundance made hospitality seem natural, while in Kaliningrad, food felt like an indulgence. I started to question: What does it mean to provide comfort in an area with few resources? When everything around you seems cold, how can you create warmth? Perhaps, even at that time, I was starting to realize that hospitality is more than simply what's on the table; it's also about the purpose of it, finding ways to feed others when you have little to offer.

I remember the trips to the Kaliningrad forests with my father. He taught me to identify the mushrooms that grew there, a skill that became one of the few moments of bliss I grasped in a place that often felt like it was fading away. We returned home with baskets full of mushrooms, their earthy aroma filling the kitchen as my father sautéed them in butter. These moments, small and fleeting, became a source of solace—a reminder that even in the barren landscape of Kaliningrad, there was still something to be found, still something worth holding on to.

After we resettled in the Kaliningrad region, my parents, with a quiet sorrow they rarely expressed, decided it was best for me to live with Babushka in Vilnius. Life there, they believed, held more promise—cleaner streets, steadier rhythms, a gentler existence. My brother remained with them in Kaliningrad, while I was entrusted to Babushka's care. For several years, she became both guardian and guide. My parents visited when they could, but those visits were infrequent, somewhat spectral—brief flickers of familial connection in a life increasingly shaped by my grandmother's quiet discipline, worn hands, unwavering presence.

Lithuania, with its rolling green hills, lakes, and forests, remained a place of abundance, a stark contrast to the desolate industrial landscape of Kaliningrad. When I had visited, I felt the tempo of the land beneath my feet—its seasons, its cycles, its deep connection to the past. The land of the Kaliningrad region, by comparison, appeared disconnected, as if it had forgotten how to grow and how to thrive. Yet, in those still moments with my father—picking mushrooms, savoring the fruits of the earth—I felt a fleeting connection to something larger than myself.

By the time I turned twelve, the world around me was beginning to shift. The political landscape of the Soviet Union, once a fixture in our lives, began to fracture. The whispers of independence from the Baltic republics grew louder, and even in the tranquil forests of Kaliningrad, there was a sense of unrest. The future, once so certain, felt uncertain, fragile even. As the Soviet Union dissolved, so, too, did the sense of stability that marked my childhood. The seasons, once predictable, became harbingers of change—of a world on the brink of transformation. And I, too, began to sense that something within me was shifting, that the rituals of childhood would soon be left behind, replaced by a future I had yet to understand.

In those final years, as the warm allure of summer gave way to the cooler touch of fall, I held on to the rituals that shaped me. The aroma of freshly baked cookies, the warmth of Babushka's hand in mine, and the serene peace of the dacha—they remained, even as the world around me changed. The connection to the land, to food, to family, always remained a part of me, no matter what the future held.

Though I didn't fully appreciate it at the time, my grandmother's sagacity, her strength, and her wisdom in both the kitchen and in life stayed with me. She showed me that food isn't only survival—it's connection. It's sharing the fruits of your labor with those you adore, breaking bread together, and creating something that nourishes both body and soul. My grandmother's "cult for food," as my mother called it, was the seed that eventually grew into my own passion for hospitality—a passion rooted in the idea that food is a language of love, a way of showing the world who you are.

I believe that hospitality, at its core, is a benevolent act—a way of offering nourishment not simply to the body but to the spirit and mind. Through food and beverage, I strive to make people feel welcomed, valued, and cared for, as my grandmother made me feel every day of my life.

CHAPTER 3

The Soul of Hospitality

The air in my grandmother's kitchen was always thick with warmth—both from the steam rising off the stove and from the unspoken devotion that infused every movement. She never spoke of hospitality as a virtue, never pontificated on its moral gravity, yet in her silent, inconspicuous choreography of preparing a meal, she offered lessons that words cannot fully encompass: the way she laid out the tablecloth as if it were a sacred ritual, the way she arranged the plates not for necessity but for grace. To her, food was not sustenance alone—it was a gesture, a bridge, an unspoken assurance that someone was welcome, that the walls of her home were permeable to those in need of warmth.

Hospitality is not a performance, nor is it reserved for formal occasions. It lives in the everyday—the way you pour tea for the neighbor who stops by to borrow sugar, the way you fashion an entire feast from seemingly nothing if an unexpected guest appears at the door. There is no hesitation, no sense of burden, only an unshakable certainty that no one should ever feel like an outsider. To turn someone away, to allow them to feel like an imposition, is unthinkable.

From my grandmother, I learned that hospitality is not a service but a way of being—a philosophy woven into the fabric of life. There are unspoken rules, but they are not rigid dictates. They are instincts passed down through generations, absorbed as naturally as breath: A guest should never sense the effort behind their welcome. Food should be abundant, not merely in quantity but in spirit. It does not only fill the stomach but nourishes deeper. The host serves first and waits until every need is met.

More than the customs, it is the undercurrent of care, the wordless sentiment behind each gesture, that defines true hospitality. I did not know it then, but the time I spent at my grandmother's table defined the course of my life. Her discipline, her ceaseless devotion to those around her, and her refusal to let difficulty dilute the generosity of her spirit—all of these shaped me. Her Russian roots carried with them a sense of obligation, an understanding that nothing in life is given freely, that everything must be earned through persistence. Hardship is never an excuse for withholding warmth; struggle does not absolve one from the duty of caring for others. It is only later, through years spent in the hotel management industry, I come to realize her lessons have quietly become the foundation upon which I build my understanding of the world.

Some of my earliest and most cherished memories are of my birthdays, marked not by gifts but by the way my grandmother turned the day into a celebration of familial devotion. She prepared a table so abundant it appeared as if she had been preparing for weeks—Olivier salad, delicate *blini*, Russian-style cutlets, and the ever-present *holodets*, a dish of jellied meat I could never bring myself to enjoy but understood as part of our tradition. It was not simply about food but about creating a moment that lingered in memory, a ritual of belonging. I understand now that it was never indulgence but presence. Through my grandmother's meticulous attention to detail and the precise arrangement of the dishes, she was not only providing nourishment, she was also establishing a foundation of memory, continuity, and something that endured beyond her lifetime.

Through those I meet, I come to understand that hospitality is both universal and yet entirely distinct in its manifestations. Each culture carries its own interpretation of what it means to welcome another, and in these variations, I find a richness that deepens my understanding of human connection.

Germans—theirs is hospitality in quiet efficiency, an attentiveness that never overwhelms but anticipates. The French transform hospitality into an art form, a performance of refinement where every gesture, every carefully poured glass of wine, is an offering of mastery. The English hold fast to restraint—hospitality is understated, an unobtrusive but unwavering presence, a politeness that reassures without ostentation.

Then, there are the Russians. Hospitality is grand, extravagant, and unyielding. To enter a Russian home is to surrender to abundance. Tables groan under the mass of dishes, vodka flows without hesitation, and to refuse food is nearly an insult. Weddings last for days, punctuated by endless toasts, each speech prolonged more than the last, a demonstration not only of festivity but of commitment to collective joy.

The motion of hospitality is not a choice but a necessity, a reflection of soul and character. You feed guests not because they are hungry, but because in feeding them, you affirm their belonging. It is this same sense of belonging that overwhelmed me when I attended my first Indian wedding. I did not understand, at first, why the groom paraded through the streets on a towering elephant, why the music swelled as guests danced in an unrestrained celebration. The *baraat*—a procession as much about felicity as it honors tradition—felt surreal to me. Still, as I watched, as I was pulled into the thrumming hum of it all, I began to understand. Hospitality is immersion; it is the invitation not in the mere guise of observing but in participation, being absorbed into a world not your own, and for a fleeting moment, belonging within it.

I see this same distinct principle when I serve high tea for the first time. In the high tea ceremony, hospitality embodies precision, a meticulous ballet of service where no detail is overlooked. The teacups must be placed at a precise angle; the scones arranged in a hierarchy of delicacy. There is no excess, no unbridled warmth spilling over the edges—only a carefully measured elegance, a welcome that exists in the refinement of the details. It is no less genuine, but it is restrained and controlled, a testament to the idea that hospitality can be felt as keenly in a gentle nod of acknowledgment as in a lavish display of abundance.

Different cultures cultivate hospitality in manners both refined and deeply resonant. In places where hierarchy is ingrained, such as India or parts of the Middle East, hospitality is inseparable from respect and reverence. A guest's status dictates the order of service, the manner of greeting, and the very arrangement of seating. In cultures that prioritize collectivism, such as Japan, hospitality is woven into the structure of community—small, deliberate gestures communicate care, and to impose is unthinkable. In highly individualistic societies, such as the United States, hospitality often leans toward the transactional, a practiced warmth that may or may not extend beyond the moment of exchange.

Yet, hospitality is not only culture or service; it is a way of seeing the world. It is an instinct to offer before being asked, to anticipate without expectation of return. It is what lingers when the meal is finished, when the guests have gone, when the space left behind still hums with the memory of presence. It is this essence—the intangible, the unspoken—that I will carry forward from my grandmother's house as I move beyond serving, beyond hosting, into something deeper.

Perhaps the greatest lesson is not in the husk of offering hospitality but in living it. To extend it not only in dining rooms and celebrations but in understated moments, in everyday encounters, in the way we move through the world. As I step forward, I know that hospitality will not only continue to shape my work—it defines my way of being. With this understanding, I turn toward what lies ahead, where hospitality is no longer a practice but a philosophy—one that extends far beyond the table and into life itself.

CHAPTER 4

The Day of the Parade

There are moments in life when the air itself seems to change, when the world you've known slips away without warning, and you are left grasping at fragments of a past that no longer holds any promise of return. That day, when Lithuania declared its independence and the Parade of Hope marched through the streets of Vilnius, was one such moment. It wasn't only a change in the political landscape; it was the unraveling of the world I had known, a shift that, in time, fractured the essential foundation of my existence. Looking back, I see now that the world around me was on the verge of transformation. At the time, I was living full-time with my grandmother in Vilnius, my home since grade two. Now in grade four, I was caught in the humdrum of daily life, unaware that I was standing on the threshold of something far greater than the schoolwork and the familiar streets of the city. The world I had known, the routine of everyday life, was about to be overturned.

On the day of the parade, the atmosphere was thick with anticipation. There was a sense of both pride and tension in the air, as if everyone felt something monumental was unfolding. Yet, for my grandmother, there was fear—fear of what was to come. We didn't see the violence firsthand, but we heard it. From her apartment, I heard faint echoes of gunfire and the distant rumble of tanks rolling through the streets. The political shifts in Lithuania were no longer abstract; they were real, and they were happening right outside our door. The peaceful days of Lithuania's Soviet rule, of being part of the USSR, were slipping away. What had once been a daily reality for me, something I took for granted, was now being questioned—as the very identity of Lithuania itself was in flux.

My grandmother was no stranger to fear. She, a Russian woman whose life had been irrevocably shaped by the horrors of war, carried with her a legacy of silence and survival. Her past was a tangle of memories woven together by fear, secrets, and the unspoken truths that shaped her worldview.

Most pressing of these truths was my grandfather's heritage. My grandpa, a decorated World War II veteran, was Jewish, but that fact had been concealed from me and my brother until we were almost sixteen. My grandmother's fear was not only rooted in the political instability of the present, but in the legacy of repression that had haunted her life—a legacy tied to the secrecy of my grandfather's ethnicity. To her, it was not merely the shifting political tides in Lithuania—it was the ever-present fear of being discovered and the danger that came from a truth too dangerous to be spoken aloud.

As Lithuania's independence loomed, the fear that had once been an unruffled murmur in her life grew into a loud, insistent presence. The fear had become more than the tanks on the street or the uncertainty of the political future; it was the specter of a past she diligently attempted to ignore. The prospect of change, of losing control, felt too much like the fear of a past that nearly destroyed her. It was then she made a decision that altered the course of my life forever. It wasn't simply the upheaval in Lithuania that prompted her; it was the unbearable burden of history, the fear of what could happen if I remained in Vilnius. So, with trembling hands and a soul weighed down by the burden of her past, she sent me away. She wasn't simply sending me to another place—she was evacuating me from looming uncertainty to a land that felt stable though foreign. To the Kaliningrad region, to Yuzhnyy, where my parents awaited.

I felt urgency in every one of her movements, the sense that time was running out. There were no long goodbyes, only hurried packing, an unspoken understanding that we were parting for reasons deeper than either of us could explain. She was sending me toward something unknown, a world I could not fathom.

As I boarded the train, I did not know what awaited me, but I knew that nothing would be the same when I returned. The train ride itself was uneventful, but it felt profound. As Vilnius receded from view, I couldn't shake the feeling that I wasn't only leaving my grandmother behind—I was leaving behind a version of myself, a life that was slipping away even as I moved forward. I was stepping into an uncertain future; one I could not control.

Though the political unrest in Lithuania did not cease with my departure, I was far removed from it. The declaration of independence would soon come, and with it, the struggles that shaped Lithuania's future, but for me, in the distant Kaliningrad region, the world felt still. Yuzhnyy, a military outpost, felt quieter, the winds of change less immediate, less violent. Yet it was still a transition, a move away from everything I had known. It was a world that seemed strange, even though it was not far from home. I was thrust into a life that felt distant and foreign, with a family scattered by time and circumstance.

In Yuzhnyy, my parents were waiting for me, but they were not the same people I remembered. The space between us felt too vast, the bond too fragile. It was not a bad place, but it wasn't home. The people were different, the culture unfamiliar. My new school, my new surroundings—all of it felt alien. I had been torn from the world I knew and thrown into a new one where everything felt uncertain, unwelcoming, like a fog refusing to lift.

Amid all this unpredictability, something subtle changed. My parents, once distant and disconnected from my life, were now present.

We began the slow, tentative process of reconnecting. My brother and I, though still separate in many ways, began to rebuild the bridge that once linked us. It wasn't a grand reunion, but rather a gentle coming together, piece by piece. We shared in small moments—a meal together, a conversation here and there—and through these ordinary acts, I felt the beginnings of something like belonging.

During this time, my aunt, not living with us in Yuzhnyy, sent me a gift: a bright pink and fluorescent green jacket. It appeared frivolous to some, but to me, it became a symbol of my individuality in a place that felt like it swallowed all personal identity. That jacket, loud and bright, became my shield, a way to keep something of myself in a world that sought to define me by its terms. It was a small gesture, but it meant everything to me. The jacket became more than a simple piece of clothing; it became an emblem of how I was beginning to navigate this strange new world.

The world I left behind, with its familiar streets and faces, felt so far away, yet the warmth of those memories clung to me. I missed Lithuania—the forests, the dachas, the sense of home. Yet as time passed, I understood that home was no longer defined by geography. It was something deeper, something formed by the bonds of family, of compassion, and of the tender hospitality that tied us. Yuzhnyy, for all its bluntness, began to feel like the place where I could start anew. There, in the midst of all the uncertainty and unfamiliarity, I learned that love, connection, and family were the things that gave a place meaning.

> *In the midst of uncertainty and unfamiliarity, love, connection, and family are what gives a place meaning.*

In time, I realized home wasn't defined as a place where you lived; it was defined by the people you lived with. Home was shared moments, placid support, and warmth of togetherness. As the days and months passed, I found myself growing into this new reality, trying to reconcile the two worlds I had come from. Lithuania, with its fight for independence, and Yuzhnyy, with its reticent remnants of a Soviet past, were the bookends of my life, each shaping me in different ways. Yet here, in Yuzhnyy, I began to understand what it meant to rebuild—a home, an identity, a family. The fractures that once seemed insurmountable were slowly healing, and I found a new sense of belonging. Yuzhnyy was my next chapter, not simply a place to exist, but a place where I reshaped my understanding of family, identity, and home. A place of transition, a place of rebirth. The journey that had begun with a train ride would take me farther, but it was marked by this time of transformation, this reticent redefinition of what it meant to belong.

CHAPTER 5

A Bond Beyond Borders

On my last day of high school, the gravity of the moment sank in. The light from the spring sun streamed through the classroom windows, casting long shadows across the worn wooden desks. The fragrance of lilacs wafted through the air, and I found myself transported to another time—one that felt more distant with every passing second. It had been seven years since I left Vilnius, and though so much had happened since, it all passed in a blur, as if time folded in on itself. The days stretched long, but the years vanished quickly. Outside, the world hummed with the noise of planes flying overhead, a constant reminder that life moved forward, shifting beyond my grasp. The past, despite all my efforts to hold on to it, faded. I was there, in that classroom, in the center of Yuzhnyy, the military outpost nestled in the Kaliningrad region, where the five-story concrete apartment buildings rose like sentinels around the U-shaped school.

The apartments loomed over the yard, silent witnesses to all the years I had spent here. The cadence of military life, cold and regimented, was the backdrop to my existence, but as I sat there, on my final day, I felt the place had become smaller. The expansive grounds that once gave the impression of stretching out infinitely now feel more contained, confined within the boundaries of the outpost. It was a place I could no longer reach, no matter how much I longed to hold on to it.

Yuzhnyy was home for so many years—a place where we lived and survived. The gray, concrete buildings and the military routines shaped every moment of our lives. Still, as I sat there, with the classroom bathed in warm light, the world outside felt like a distant echo, no longer mine to touch. My mind drifted back to the years we spent in Azerbaijan, a land so strikingly different. The desert stretched out in every direction, harsh and unforgiving, but it was there, in that land of extremes, that I learned to appreciate the small moments of beauty.

> ***In a land of extremes, I learned to appreciate small moments of beauty.***

Our yard, with its fruit trees—apricots, pomegranates, and figs—was an oasis, a burst of life against the barren landscape. The apricots, soft and blond, were little pockets of summer, so sweet it seemed they had absorbed the very essence of the sun. The pomegranates, their deep red seeds bursting with juice, stained our fingers with the depths of life. The figs, with their smooth skin, were an abundant gift in a place that often felt stripped of luxury. Those fruits weren't simply food—they were life, offered by the earth. Gifts from the land, each bite a small treasure; I can still taste them, remember the way they felt in my hands.

I recall too how my father would always bring home something extraordinary. One of his most cherished gifts was Beluga caviar, a luxury that few in the world enjoy, let alone a family living in a military outpost. In Azerbaijan, with the Caspian Sea nearby, my father often returned with gallon-sized jars filled with these black pearls harvested from the waters. We sat together as a family, eating the caviar on thick slices of white bread with butter, savoring each bite as though it were a moment that could never be repeated. I didn't realize at the time how rare and genuinely special those moments were. I didn't understand the privilege of tasting Beluga caviar whenever my father brought it home. It wasn't until we left Azerbaijan, moving far away to Yuzhnyy, that I grasped the significance of those indulgences.

In the Kaliningrad region, caviar was something we couldn't afford. It was a reminder of a time and place that felt distant, like a world beyond reach. My father's rare gifts, like caviar, weren't solely about the luxury of the food; they were a connection to something bigger, something outside the borders of our small world. Yet, the greatest gift my father gave me wasn't the caviar or the fruit trees. It was the sense of adventure, the trust he instilled in me.

> ***The greatest gift my father gave me was his sense of adventure.***

In Azerbaijan, he took me far from the boundary of our home out to the vastness of the Caspian Sea. I clung to him as we swam, his strong arms holding me, keeping me safe as we ventured farther into the water. The shore became a blur, the cold waves washing over us. Still, there was no fear—only trust. Trust that my father, the one figure in my life who had always been a symbol of strength, would bring me back to safety.

My father didn't often express his affection with words, but he showed it through his actions: the way he carried me through the waters, the way he brought us treasures from afar. Each moment was his way of telling us we were part of something bigger than our small world. It wasn't only the caviar—it was the experiences he shared with us, the adventures that carried us beyond the outpost boundaries.

My mother, too, shaped our lives in a quieter way. She didn't give us extravagant gifts or take us on grand adventures, but her love and care were constant, a steady influence in life. She rose early every day to ensure we had what we needed. It was her steady presence, her ability to create a home even in the most uncertain circumstances that gave us the strength to keep going. I think of the jars of vegetables that my grandmother sent from Lithuania—preserved from her garden, a link to the past, a reminder that family was always there, even from across the miles. These jars of vegetables were more than food; they were a lifeline, a comfort when things were scarce.

I can still feel the warmth of those winters in Yuzhnyy, when the snow fell in thick, quiet blankets, covering the world in a stillness that gave the impression it stretched on forever. Inside our small apartment, there was always warmth—not from the stove, but from the fondness and laughter we shared as a family. I remember sitting at the table with my mother, drinking tea, listening to the wind howl outside, and feeling safe, like we had everything we needed, even when the world was cold and harsh.

Then, there was my brother, the one who shared this life with me. Together we raced down the snow-covered hills behind the hangars, our laughter echoing through the cold air. The wind stung our faces, but we didn't care. In those moments, there was nothing but joy. It was in these simple moments, in the shared joy of childhood, when our bond deepened. As his older sister, I always felt the pressure of responsibility. Even before he was born, I had this fierce sense of protectiveness. I talked to my mother's belly, my voice filled with excitement and anticipation, imagining what it would be like to finally have him in the world.

Once he was born, and my parents worked long overnight shifts at the base, I stepped in without hesitation. I tried to cook for him, though I wasn't always successful. The meals were simple—clumsy at first—but I did my best. I was his protector, his caretaker, and he, in turn, looked up to me with eyes filled with admiration. I felt it in the way he watched me, his small face full of trust. His veneration for me, so pure and unwavering, only deepened my sense of responsibility. I wanted to be everything for him: the sister, the mother, the shield. There was a bond between us, not only through blood but also through shared moments and shared experiences.

In those quiet moments when I tucked him into bed, I realized I was shaping his world as much as he was shaping mine. We grew up together, but in many ways, I felt as though I had grown into a role I hadn't anticipated—the one of protector, the one who took care of him, and the one who helped him navigate the small but meaningful moments of life in the military outpost of Yuzhnyy, with its cold concrete buildings and buzz of military life.

This was our home, but it was also a place where we built our own little world—a world of warmth and familiarity. Every visit from friends or family was a welcome event. We'd sit around the table, the aroma of tea filling the air, and share stories of the outside world—of places we'd never been and might never see. Russian hospitality was woven into the fabric of our home, with my mother always ensuring there was enough food, enough tea, and enough warmth for everyone. It was this tradition, this ritual, that marked so many of our evenings. The laughter, the quiet conversations, the endless drinks—it all felt like a constant thread that bound us together in this otherwise foreign and isolated place.

My memories of Yuzhnyy are colored by these moments of connection, the warmth of conviviality in the face of the cold, and the bonds we forged with one another. It was in this place where I learned the true value of family—togetherness. It was here where my brother and I bonded over small acts of kindness, shared laughter, and the quiet realization that we were always there for each other, no matter what.

As I sat in the classroom on my last day of high school, I reflected on how the moments—the caviar, the fruit trees, the winters in

Yuzhnyy, the simple moments with family—shaped me. They became part of who I was, treasures I carried with me long after I left that place. These experiences were the bond connecting me to the past, reminders of where I came from and of the love always at the nucleus of my story.

As high school drew to a close, I found myself uncertain about what came next, yet resolute in my determination to shape my future. Dreams of adventure and experiences beyond the familiar streets of Kaliningrad lingered in my mind, though they felt distant and elusive, like stars in the night sky. At that moment, those aspirations appeared evanescent, abstract, and intangible. Little did I know, life has a curious way of unfolding in ways we least expect. While I couldn't yet foresee where my path would lead after graduation, there was an undeniable sense that something transformative waited beyond the horizon. The magnitude of what lay ahead was a mystery, but it was clear that soon, the world would expand before me.

CHAPTER 6

The Great Leap

May 2000. The moment I stepped out of the New Yorker Hotel in Manhattan, everything I thought I knew about the world shattered. It wasn't simply the sheer size of the city, the overpowering noise, or the relentless pace of life—it was something that transcended the surface, something intangible that gripped my soul. The cacophony of sounds—horns honking, people shouting, the rhythmic pounding of footsteps against the concrete—was deafening. The air felt dense with energy, electric and unnerving, as though the very streets were alive and moving around me. The smell of street food mingled with the exhaust of cars, a pungent yet oddly intoxicating fragrance. I had never seen anything like it before. The towering skyscrapers stretched endlessly into the sky, blocking out the sun and giving the streets a shadowed, claustrophobic quality. It was as though the city itself was a giant, pulsating organism, breathing and living in a way I had never imagined.

I was so small in comparison. A stranger in a strange land, overwhelmed by a world that felt too vast to navigate and too fast to comprehend. Yet it wasn't merely the size or the noise; it was the people. I had never seen so many different faces—so many different colors—in one place. People from every corner of the world coexisted on these sidewalks, speaking languages I didn't understand, wearing clothes I had never seen. There were Black, Hispanic, Asian, and Caucasian faces, their expressions a mix of determination, exhaustion, and focus as they rushed past me in a blur. It was a celebration of diversity unlike anything I had ever encountered in my hometown of Kaliningrad.

Growing up, I had been surrounded by people who were mostly ethnically Russian, with white skin like mine, speaking the same language, living in a world that felt small but safe and familiar. Here, I was in the minority, a foreigner. It wasn't only the visual difference that stood out—it was how out of place I felt in this city. There was no space for me to breathe. The streets, though filled with life, felt cold and indifferent. I didn't know how to navigate them or where to go next. I was another face in the crowd, trying to hold on to something familiar, but there was nothing to hold on to.

My English, though passable in theory, was shaky at best. The rapid-fire conversations happening around me were incomprehensible. I could articulate simple sentences, yet here, the words eluded me like sand through my fingers. I barely understood the street signs, let alone the voices around me. The city was an alien landscape, with its own rhythm, its own language, and its own rules. I kept walking, unsure of where I was going, but too afraid to stop. I was terrified of standing still, of being exposed. So, I walked. I moved through the streets, searching for something, though I didn't know what that something was.

Amid all the chaos, I wasn't alone. Eugene and Natalia—two of the closest people I had with me on this journey—were as overwhelmed as I was. We had arrived together as part of the J-1 Work and Travel Program, a dream come true when we signed up. The program promised us work experience and a glimpse into American life, but nothing prepared us for the full magnitude of the reality we faced.

Eugene and Natalia, unlike me, had managed to learn more English. Eugene, a reserved and thoughtful person, was somewhere between Natalia's fluency and my own struggles. He had a way of thinking before speaking, which was useful in a place where everything was new. Natalia, conversely, was confident and more comfortable with the language. She tried her best to navigate the streets and help me find my way, but even with their better English skills, we were all lost in one way or another.

Our journey had begun long before stepping foot in Manhattan. We arrived at JFK Airport in the early hours. The city was asleep, darkness stretching long over the streets. As the plane touched down, the urgency of our arrival felt distant. The vastness of the sky above blurred the reality of the moment. The airport was dormant—a brief respite before the chaos—as we navigated through customs and baggage claim. It was four in the morning, and the exhaustion of the flight weighed on me like a physical burden. My eyes were heavy, but a part of me was vividly awake, anxious to see what awaited us in this foreign new world.

We were ushered into a bus with others from the J-1 program. The seats were mostly empty, save for a few scattered bodies, all of us foreigners, eyes glazed with anticipation. The journey from the airport to our hotel was surreal. The streets of New York were deserted at that hour, silent except for the occasional hum of passing cars and the whir of the bus engine, but the city's lights—thousands of them—flashed around us like stars, flickering against the black sky, bright and alive. Each street sign, building, and reflection danced in the dark, a shimmering promise of something unknown. It was hard to comprehend what I was seeing, as though the very city was too large to grasp in one moment.

When we arrived at the hotel, I felt an unnerving disorientation. The space was small and temporary, a tiny corner of the city where we could rest, but only for a few hours before the whirlwind began again. The schedule was relentless—we were expected to attend an orientation with hundreds of other J-1 participants at eight o'clock.

As the city thrummed outside our window, I lay awake, unable to process the magnitude of it all. The strain of fear and the excitement of adventure collided within me, creating a cocktail of emotions I could not yet name. The noise outside never ended—horns blaring, sirens wailing, people shouting—but inside, everything felt still and tranquil. The night sky held a mystery. It was so different from the night sky in Kaliningrad, where the stars burned bright, crisp, and cold. Here, the stars were veiled, obscured by the city's light. It was as though the sky had been stolen from me, hidden behind the brilliance of the city below.

In those moments, I felt a deep, aching isolation. Kaliningrad, though small and remote, had always been home. I knew the streets, the sounds, and the faces. I could walk through the city without a second thought. In New York, I was a stranger. The innate essence of the city seemed designed to overwhelm. It was as if the universe had pushed me out of my comfort zone, telling me there was no going back, no returning to the familiarity I had known. Still, I couldn't deny the excitement stirring in my chest. New York was not my home, but it was the stop before Maine, the place that later came to feel like a second home. For better or for worse, this was where my journey had begun.

The next morning, as I stepped out of the hotel and onto the streets, it all came crashing down on me—the scope of what I had done, the magnitude of my decision to leave Kaliningrad behind. The city had transformed from a mere dream into a vibrant, living entity. The noise, the people, the constant motion—it felt like the heaviness of the world was pressing against my shoulders. I felt small and insignificant in the face of it all. The feeling of being a tiny speck in a vast and sprawling universe overwhelmed me.

Yet, there was also something else—something deeper. I felt a gentle surge of gratitude. This was my chance, and there was no turning back now. Before this dizzying moment in New York City, my life had been a journey of growth in Kaliningrad—a place that felt both like home and a springboard to the world. Kaliningrad, with its historic blend of Russian and German influences, had given me everything I needed to take this leap.

From an early age, I was drawn to roles of leadership. In high school, I was known for my discipline and drive—captain of the ROTC club and head of the topography team. I thrived on challenges, eager to prove not only my capabilities but my worth. Whether I was marching in competitions, navigating the forests with a map I could barely read, or role-playing military exercises, I poured myself into every pursuit. These weren't activities—they were glimpses into a part of me that longed for direction, for purpose. At the heart of it, I wasn't chasing recognition—I was searching for meaning. I wanted to guide others, to forge paths for myself and for those around me.

At the end of high school, I turned my sights toward the law. It seemed, on the surface, like a natural extension of that desire—to lead, to protect, to stand for something larger than myself. Yet something in me resisted. The path of law demanded a level of dispassionate rigor that felt at odds with the kind of service I yearned for. I wondered if the courtroom would distance me from the people I most wanted to help.

The pivotal point came during a trip to Krasnaya Polyana, a picturesque mountain resort near Sochi. My mother and I decided to take a break from the pressures of high school exams and university plans. The region, with its breathtaking landscapes and deep history, would change my life. We spent five days hiking the mountains with a group of people from all across Russia. The days were exhausting—hard work—but the reward was beyond words. The views of the valleys, peaks, and forests were unlike anything I had ever seen. At night, we gathered around campfires, shared stories, sang songs to the strumming of a guitar, and laughed at challenges we had faced on the trail. The simplicity of the experience, the camaraderie, and the way people from different walks of life came together made me realize how much I loved connecting with others. I didn't feel called to law; I felt called to help people in a different way—to listen to their stories and create experiences that change lives.

After the hike, we spent another five days by the Black Sea, indulging in local cuisine, dancing the night away, and soaking in the vibrant atmosphere of the area. I was seventeen years old, and the world felt like a boundless sea of possibilities. My mother, who had always supported me quietly but fiercely, was by my side. In those mountains, I saw her in a different light. She endured so much in her life—losing her parents at a young age, surviving as an orphan, and navigating a challenging career in the construction industry where she often had to manage people twice her age. My mother had always been my unwavering pillar of support, but in those mountains, I saw her vulnerability, her love, and the deep, unspoken longing she had for me to succeed.

At night, as we looked up at the star-filled skies, drinking tea with local desserts, I realized how fortunate I was to have her in my corner. She had never imagined I would leave Russia for a foreign land, but in her atman, she believed anything was possible. Her belief in me helped me decide to change my career path and pursue hospitality. It was a decision that shaped my future.

> *Because my mother believed in me, I changed my life.*

Returning to Kaliningrad, I enrolled in the newly established hospitality program at Kaliningrad State University. It felt like an entirely new chapter. The program, still in its infancy, was everything I needed to take that next step toward my future, even if it was uncharted territory. The true journey had begun.

Kaliningrad State University (now Immanuel Kant Baltic Federal University) was the perfect place for me to begin this new chapter of my life. The university had a fantastic history, stretching back to the sixteenth century when it was known as the University of Königsberg. While it was arduous to ignore the magnitude of history, it also served as a source of inspiration. It was here that I met Eugene. Eugene, with his advanced English skills and patient demeanor, would become one of my closest friends. Together, we navigated the challenges of the program.

It was at Kaliningrad State University where I genuinely began to understand the path I had chosen—a path far beyond the borders of Russia. The opportunity to study abroad in Sweden during my second year exposed me to a more developed hospitality industry, and I quickly saw how much I could learn from countries with a long history in tourism. By my third year—now the year 2000, three years after graduating high school—I learned about the J-1 Work and Travel Program, a program that offered firsthand experience in the US. I applied immediately, eager to see what awaited me beyond the borders of Russia. The J-1 program felt like the perfect next step, a chance to experience the American hospitality industry and culture. For all that though, when I arrived in New York, I quickly realized that nothing prepared me for the challenge ahead.

In that blur of the first days—surrounded by unfamiliar words, strangers, and the sheer force of the city—what sustained me was not confidence or skill, but something far more enduring. In that disorienting first day in New York—when the noise refused to relent, when even the sky felt lost behind the buildings, it wasn't ambition or courage that kept me moving. It was memory.

Not of place, but of presence.

Of my mother, walking beside me in the mountains of Krasnaya Polyana.

Of her silence, which said more than any speech.

Of her belief in me, quiet and absolute, when I hadn't yet earned it.

She had no map for this journey. She hadn't left, hadn't crossed oceans, but she understood longing. She understood sacrifice. She had weathered loss without bitterness, endured work that asked too much and gave too little, and still, she chose care over complaint. She never pushed me toward the unknown, but when the unknown arrived, she did not hesitate.

It was her presence—steady, patient—that gave shape to my leap. She did not hold me back, even as I drifted beyond what she had known. She gave no grand advice. Only space. Only trust.

Without her, I might never have strayed from the path. I might have chosen safety over uncertainty, structure over discovery.

But she let me go, and in doing so, gave me everything.

She is the breath in every risk I take.

The calm beneath the chaos.

The love that needs no witness.

She is my home.

She is my wind.

Even now, from across oceans, she steadies me.

CHAPTER 7

The Journey Begins

The chaos of Port Authority had a surreal, unrelenting tempo. It was impossible to look anywhere without the sense that one's eyes were being pulled in every direction. It felt as though the world had broken down into fragments, as if some higher force had taken a hammer and shattered all sense of order into a thousand disjointed pieces. I stood with Eugene and Natalia, all of us caught in this flood of bodies and sound, unable to find our bearings. We had made it to the station.

We had arrived in New York, finally, after the long hours of travel, after the time we spent imagining this exact moment, thinking how this journey—our journeys—would unfold. At this point, now, with the noise of a thousand conversations and footsteps clashing together, it was as though all our expectations collided with the dizzying pulse of the city. Like being in the heart of an ant colony, everything swarming around us, moving without any discernible pattern, a ceaseless stream of individuals, all seemingly unaware of their shared location or their intended destination. There was something surreal in how each individual seemed absorbed in their own realm, how it felt like no one was genuinely aware of the others, though we were all bound in this vast network.

So, there we were, three souls in the middle of it all, paralyzed. Where to go next? Where was the line? Where was the booth, the ticket counter? The questions bounced in my mind, but the answers never quite materialized. The overhead lights flickered, bathing the terminal in cold, unwelcoming light, while the occasional speaker blared, making announcements that only added to the general confusion. It was a moment of stillness inside of the whirlwind. I felt my pulse racing, my heart thumping in my chest, but none of us moved. Too much was happening at once to absorb it all, too much to process.

I glanced at Eugene, who looked as lost as I felt. His brow furrowed in frustration; his hands buried deep into the pockets of his coat. I sensed his impatience, the desire to move on, but we were stuck—trapped in the noise and the chaos, as though our feet were glued to the floor. Then, I turned to Natalia. Her face was indecipherable, a slight wrinkle in her brow betraying the same confusion rooted in me. Yet, beneath it all, I also saw something else—something tender in her eyes, a glimmer of marvel. Despite the disorientation and the fear that this city had somehow swallowed us, she was taking it all in.

We needed to do something—anything. Slowly, almost unwillingly, our feet moved. Step by step, we made our way through the throngs of people, dodging travelers, maneuvering around luggage carts, squinting in the haze of voices and indistinct figures. Finally, after what felt like an unending time of aimless wandering, we stumbled on the line for the Greyhound counter. It was there, hidden amid the confusion, a line that stretched toward the far wall, yet it felt like the most miraculous discovery in the world. I glanced at Eugene, who bobbed his head with a sigh of relief. For a moment, it felt as though the city had stopped solely for us. The clamor, the bustle—everything faded away, leaving only the enigmatic, comforting murmur of the line in front of us, the mundane act of waiting. We weren't entirely sure what to expect from this bus trip. It felt too simple, too ordinary.

A ride to Bangor, Maine. I noticed the topography changing as we drove through, but there was something deeper in the idea of leaving the city behind, something primal. Perhaps it was the fact that I had lived all my life in an endless buzz of noise and movement, in cities without end. The notion of getting on a bus and fleeing this insanity—of heading toward something quieter, something cleaner—felt like the expel of a breath I hadn't realized I'd been holding for years.

The line moved slowly but steadily, and soon enough we had our tickets in hand. Eugene, Natalia, and I found our seats on the bus, a unified silence falling over us as we settled into the plush seats, a silence I found strangely comforting in contrast to the world we left behind. The bus's engine sputtered to life, and I watched through the window as Port Authority grew smaller and smaller, a beast retreating into the distance. Even so, New York—its pulse, its noise, its disorientation—followed us for a moment, lingering like the echo of a song half-remembered. The gray streets blurred together as the bus navigated the thick web of traffic, the buildings rising like jagged teeth around us.

The city's grip loosened as we swerved through the streets, the bus weaving through five lanes of frantic traffic, pushing its way past honking cars and taxis darting in and out, the drivers seemingly lost in their own frenzy. My anxiety dissipated as the bus surged forward, pushing through the dense, overpopulated streets, slowly but surely making its way out of the city epicenter. The chaos, the noise, the electric energy pulsing beneath the surface—those elements of New York that had unnerved us—faded into the distance, swallowed by the landscape ahead. For a second, I had the unsettling thought that maybe the city would never let us go. But no. We were already past the limits.

We crossed into New Jersey, and the transformation was striking. The buildings grew smaller, sparser. Traffic lightened, and the streets became quieter. The oppressive skyline that had dominated the view was replaced with open fields, the occasional tree dotting the roadside like welcoming figures. It was a slow unfolding, a shift in rhythm, in tempo—one moment caught in the whirlwind of urban life, and the next drifting into something simpler, something less frantic.

The landscape itself sighed, as if it, too, had been waiting for the frenzy to be left behind. The colors deepened—green pastures, flaxen fields, and turquoise hills. Even the architecture shifted, the buildings losing their steel and glass gleam, replaced with warm, homey brick and wood that spoke of time passing slowly, of patience, of spaces meant to be lived in rather than simply used. I pressed my forehead against the cold window, watching as the city fell away.

With each passing mile, I exhaled—one breath after another, letting go of the tension that had curled itself so tightly around me in the city. There was something mesmerizing in this alteration, how the earth unveiled, as though the world was preparing to show us something else. Something unhurried. Something new. As the miles rolled on, the chaos of New York seemed like a distant memory, no longer part of the world I was now beginning to understand.

We were heading toward Maine, toward Bangor, and I couldn't help but wonder what awaited us there. What would be left of us after we left the city behind? Would we still carry its echoes within us or become part of this new landscape, with wide-open skies and endless horizons? It was impossible to say. For the time, I let the quiet of the bus, the steady song of the engine, and the vast expanse of open land wash over me. It was as if we had drifted beyond time, out of the reach of the life we had once known, and were drifting toward something entirely different.

So, we began our journey, each mile taking us farther from the city and closer to something none of us could name. As the steady thrum of the bus engine faded into the background, I drifted in and out of a restless sleep. The motion of the vehicle lulled me into a disorienting, suspended state, one where the world beyond the glass seemed distant, like a dreamscape too far to reach. In that dream, the landscape blurred into something familiar yet elusive—a place not bound by time or memory but by longing.

In my dreams, I was back in my grandmother's garden, at the dacha. The redolence of earth, the cool whisper of the zephyr—so pure, so rich. The familiar purr of nature, the fluttering leaves of the birch trees. I saw the sunlight filtering through the branches, casting dappled shadows onto the dirt paths. My grandmother's voice—soft, lilting—calling to me from across the garden, her hands busy in the soil. There was peace, a timeless tranquility that connected me to some distant part of myself I didn't yet understand.

Then, as if summoned by some invisible energy, my mother appeared at the train station. I saw her on the platform, her figure so small among the swirling mass of passengers. She waved goodbye, her face a mixture of sadness and hope, her eyes bright with the unspoken understanding that this departure was something greater than a journey. It was a passage. I wanted to run back to her, to tell her I was not ready, that the world outside was too vast, too strange.

In an instant before I could move, the dream shifted again, and the Russian forest appeared, its towering trees, the birch—my favorite—standing proud in the distance. They swayed in the wind as if whispering some ancient secret I never quite grasped.

Then, as I opened my eyes, the dream evaporated, and I was jolted into reality. The world outside the window had changed. Gone were the chaotic streets of New York, replaced by the calm, sleepy charm of Bangor, Maine.

***

The bus slowed to a stop, and I blinked, trying to clear the fog of sleep from my mind. For a moment, the real world felt too heavy, too foreign, compared to the soft, lingering aftertaste of my dreams. The bright blue sky above seemed too clear; the colors too vividly intense. I felt the cool breeze against my skin as the doors of the bus creaked open, releasing us into the unknown. Excitement surged through me, but it was mixed with a deep sense of uncertainty, like stepping into a new chapter without knowing the full story. A knot formed in my stomach—the kind that accompanies change and moments of transition. I felt like an immigrant once again, although this time, it wasn't the physical distance from home that unsettled me, but the emotional distance between who I had been and who I was about to become.

I stepped off the bus, feeling a burden pressing in on me. There, in the warmth of the late afternoon sun, standing amid the small crowd, I saw her for the first time. At first, I thought she was simply another person in the ocean of unfamiliar faces. Then, as if guided by some invisible force, I found myself looking straight at her—a woman in her late fifties, but with an ageless quality that I couldn't quite place. Her white hair, so startlingly bright, caught the light as she moved. The kind of white that one only sees in the aftermath of a life well-lived, the white that isn't faded or fragile, but strong, resilient, tenacious—beautiful in a way I hadn't expected.

Despite her youthful vitality, there was something undeniably timeless about her. Her eyes, warm and welcoming, scanned the crowd with gentle curiosity, and when they met mine, I felt an immediate pull, like I had known her in another life, another world. It was impossible to put into words how she made me feel at that moment. She wasn't simply someone waiting for us to arrive; she was someone who had already opened the door to my world, someone who had already decided, with understated certainty, that she would be part of the story I had yet to write. Her smile was disarming. It wasn't forced or rehearsed, but a smile that came effortlessly, from a place of deep, implicit kindness. She radiated warmth, a presence so calming that, in that fleeting second, I felt all my uncertainty begin to dissipate. It was as if, in her glimpse, I had found a soft anchor in the storm.

"Are you all right, dear?" she asked, her voice filled with a tenderness that immediately made me feel at home, even as my heart thudded in my chest with the rawness of a life suddenly untethered.

"I ... I think so," I said, surprised by the quiver in my voice. "It's just ... a lot. It's all so new."

Her smile widened, and she reached out to give me a gentle hug. There was something in the way she held me, as though she had known me for years, as though she understood this was more than a visit—it was a new beginning. A prelude both terrifying and exhilarating, and yet, in her arms, I found an unexpected sense of peace.

"That's quite all right, dear," she murmured, pulling away and looking at me with knowing eyes. "You're safe now. You're home."

Home. I didn't understand the significance of her words at the time. How could I? Home was a distant memory, a place tucked away in a childhood that no longer existed. Then, in that moment, standing in the warm embrace of a stranger who felt like family, something shifted. I didn't know it then, but this was the onset of something I would cherish for the rest of my life.

Her name, Marilyn Cyr, was soon spoken with such affection, such reverence, that it became synonymous with everything I longed for—serenity, wisdom, zeal. For now, she was simply "Muffy," as everyone called her, and she was the first piece of the puzzle that shaped my new life.

Muffy led us to her car, a simple, well-worn vehicle that matched her—a symbol of her grounded nature, of the life she had built, far away from the world I had known. We drove through Bangor, and though the streets were unfamiliar, there was a warmth to them. The buildings were simple and sturdy, not the towering skyscrapers of New York, but something more ... human. The pace of life was slower here, more deliberate.

With Muffy by my side, the country seemed less like an alien place and more like a place where I might belong. However, as I sat quietly in the passenger seat, gazing out at the lush landscape unfolding before me, my mind returned to that peculiar moment of connection we had shared. How had I not known, in that first instant, that Muffy would become so much more than a kind woman at the bus stop? How had I not known that, over time, her name would become synonymous with family, with the kind of benevolence that only grows stronger with the years?

I didn't know it yet, but I came to understand that Muffy was not simply someone I had met on the road—she was someone I had been searching for all along. That, in itself, felt like the first step toward a homecoming I never imagined.

As we left Bangor behind, the roads shifted, stretching out toward the great expanse of Mount Desert Island. The gentle curves of the asphalt seemed poetic, as though guiding us into a different realm. I felt the vibrations of the tires against the road, but it was Muffy's voice that really pulled me into this new world.

"Mount Desert," she said, her hands steady on the wheel, her eyes occasionally glancing away from the road, "isn't a place—it's a story. A place where history and nature meet in the most extraordinary way."

She was speaking with a passion that felt both unruffled and overwhelming, as if the land itself had somehow whispered its secrets to her over the years. She went on, her words drifting easily between the history of the island and the personal connections she'd forged in her time there.

"This island, this national park, it's not just land. It's a sanctuary—one where people come to find something. Peace, most of the time, but also sometimes, a kind of clarity."

She paused, her smile wistful. "For me, it's been a place of peace, of serenity. A place where the world falls away, and I can just be."

As the Nissan Pathfinder bumped along the narrow roads, Muffy's voice filled the car, her words painting vivid pictures of the island she adored. It seemed as though every rock, every tree, every hidden inlet on Mount Desert had a story for her. The history of the land, the changing tides, the way the light fell on the water at dusk—it was as if Muffy had lived with the island so long she had absorbed its innate essence.

"Working at the Asticou Inn has been the most extraordinary chapter of my life," she said, her eyes momentarily lost in a private thought, the warmth of her smile still present. "Thirty years I've spent there, every summer, without fail. It's more than a job, you know. It's where I met so many wonderful people from all corners of the world. I used to teach history, but the work at the inn ... it's not just flowers and events. It's connecting with people, creating moments that stay with them long after they've gone."

She giggled. "That's the real magic of this place.

People may come for the tranquility, but they leave with something far deeper."

> *Connection, creating moments that last—that's real magic.*

I sensed the pride in her words, the tenderness she held for the Asticou Inn. It was a part of her, and the way she spoke of it, I could picture the grand Victorian building—its ornate architecture, the sprawling lawns that led down to the harbor.

To Muffy, it was more than a hotel; it was a living, breathing testament to the connections she fostered over the years, an extension of herself. It was there she shared countless summers with J-1 students, young souls from distant lands, and she poured all her endearment and energy into making them feel welcome, into providing a refuge they didn't even know they needed. Her laugh, full of life and unrestrained joy, permeated the car, as though the very atmosphere was lit by it. Muffy had a way of making everything seem like an adventure, even the most boring tasks, as if life itself was a joke, and the punchline was out of reach, leaving you with a sense of delighted amusement, even if you didn't quite get it.

We passed through tiny towns and dense patches of forest, and all the while, Muffy's words knitted their way into my mind like threads of a tapestry, each one adding depth and color to the picture of the place I would call home, at least for a while. The more she spoke, the more I felt the draw of this island, its history, its fables, and of Muffy herself—this woman who shaped her life into something keenly connected to the place, a place where the past lived and breathed with every passing interval. She was the keeper of its secrets, and though I couldn't yet grasp them all, I knew instinctively that in time, I would.

We turned a corner, and there it was: the Asticou Inn, standing proudly against the backdrop of the harbor, as if it had been waiting for us all along. I looked up at it, and in that instant, something in me stirred—a feeling of awe mixed with excitement but also a deep sense of peace.

As the car rolled into the parking lot, I thought not only about the inn but also of Muffy's bungalow, which she had described with affection. A small piece of paradise, she had said. I could hardly wait to see it, this retreat she created for herself—a place of refuge and respite in the middle of her busy summers, a place where history folded in on itself in the gentlest way. Still, Muffy was the true charm of this world. She exuded warmth, like the summer sun that cloaked the island in a saffron light. The way she gazed at you, as if you were the most significant person in the world. The way she made you feel like you belonged, you were part of her family, even if you were still a stranger.

Muffy never had children of her own, yet she had a way of mothering everyone around her. It wasn't simply that she welcomed you into her life—it was that she invited you to become a part of the sanctuary she had created, full of laughter, connection, and care. Even though I could barely engage in conversation at that moment, unsure how to participate in the effortless flow of words between Eugene, Natalia, and Muffy, I felt that deep connection forming inside me. It was a docile, unspoken thing, a bond being slowly built with every word Muffy said, every laugh she shared.

I listened closely, drawn like a moth to the flame of her energy and kindness, understanding that, somehow, everything was shifting within me, even as we drove the winding roads of this beautiful island. There was a transformation taking place. I was no longer the same person who had stepped off that bus in Bangor. Then, as the landscape unfolded before me, I realized that this journey, this new, alien world, would leave its mark on me. Just as Mount Desert Island had marked Muffy, just as the Asticou Inn had become a part of her, so, too, would this island become part of me.

The evening was settling in as we drove up the narrow road that wound its way to the Asticou Inn, the glow of the harbor shimmering in the distance. The sky was still warm with the last remnants of daylight, but the crispness of the night snuck in, creeping around the edges like a slow tide. The tang of salt, pine, and earth filled the air—an intoxicating mixture that promised the kind of peace you only find at the edge of the world.

As Muffy's Nissan Pathfinder made its way up the hill, I felt the tension in my body beginning to ease, a heaviness lifting as trees and winding roads enveloped us. I was still absorbing the beauty of Mount Desert Island, its wildness and serenity already feeling like a promise, one I didn't fully understand yet but was eager to learn. Muffy's voice broke through the placid, steady purr of the car, her words painting a picture of the island's powerful history. She spoke with such reverence for the place—Mount Desert Island was, after all, more than a patch of land. It was a living testament to the fortitude of nature and to the generations who had lived and worked there.

She told us of the beauty of Acadia National Park, the significance of the terrain to the inhabitants, and how it had become not simply a job, but an oasis for her, a place where she could breathe, where the chaos of the world fell away if only for a season.

"Working here," Muffy said, her eyes sparkling as she turned onto the winding road that led to the inn, "is about the people. Every summer, people from all over the world come through these doors. I meet them, I listen to their stories. I get to know them, even if only for a little while."

She laughed, the sound warm and infectious.

"It's like having a thousand little families, and every season, I get to see them come back. It's always a new adventure. You get attached. It's hard not to."

I heard the tenderness in her voice, and I found myself listening more closely than ever. There was a strength woven in her words, a unique balance that captivated me. Muffy, with her carefree laugh and effortless charm, embodied the island itself—an ever-changing landscape that, beneath its rugged exterior, was soft and full of life. Eugene and Natalia were deep in conversation with Muffy, but I found myself drifting in and out of the words, still processing everything, still mesmerized by the transformation I was going through. The landscape outside the car had already begun to shift in my mind, too. From the concrete jungle we had escaped, Mount Desert Island seemed like a remote fantasy—a place where the world didn't hurry, didn't compete. Here, there was space to breathe, to think, and in that quiet, I could already feel myself starting to take root, even though I hadn't yet fully arrived.

***

By the time we pulled up to the Asticou Inn, the harbor below us was cloaked in the soft, melancholy beauty of twilight. The Victorian architecture of the inn loomed ahead, its old bones standing proudly against the slowly darkening sky, framed by the lush greenery and gardens that Muffy had spoken of so often. It was an enchanted, surreal scene, and it took me a moment to adjust to the fact that this was now part of my existence.

We were greeted at the door, by one of the seasoned employees Thomas, with the warmth I had already come to associate with Muffy's presence—both a welcome and a promise that I was safe, I was at home. He showed us to our quarters—Hill Top, he called it, a name so simple and unpretentious yet somehow fitting for what lay ahead. The small, two-story building stood directly across the driveway from the inn, housing the staff and providing a summer retreat for the young workers. It wasn't a palace, but to me, it might as well have been.

The Hill Top porch greeted us with an unwelcome sight, a deviation from the beauty we had experienced—a mixture of empty beer cans, cigarette butts, and the odd pizza box strewn across the wooden deck as though forgotten by time itself. I suppressed a small grimace as we climbed the rickety stairs, each creak and groan of the wooden boards reminding me this wasn't exactly a hotel in the truest sense of the word. It was a place of work, of transience, where the staff passed through like leaves in the wind, leaving little trace behind but the wear and tear of their footsteps. Still, there was something charming in the disorder, something that suggested life had passed through here and left its mark—perhaps too many marks, but marks, nonetheless. This was the real world, the side of things not carefully curated or polished. It felt genuine, raw in a way that I wasn't quite ready to confront, but I already sensed it was where I belonged.

Inside, the quarters were basic but functionable. I shared a room with two other J-1s from different corners of the world—one from Poland and the other from Bulgaria. We had small, utilitarian, no-frills beds with flimsy sheets and one pillow each, and I was given the top bunk, a small nook with a window that overlooked the harbor. I felt a strange sense of camaraderie with my roommates, strangers who, like me, were going to embark on their own unparalleled journey through this summer.

I lay back on the thin mattress, exhausted but exhilarated. The day had been a series of whirlwinds, and I could feel the heaviness of it pressing down on me, pulling me toward sleep. But before I drifted into the oblivion I so desperately needed, my mind roamed back to the harbor outside the window, the scene I still pictured in vivid detail—the small boats bobbing on the water, the faint glow of light slowly disappearing as night took its rightful place. It felt like the world had paused, if only for a moment, affording me space to breathe. I felt a mysterious sense of attachment already, as though Northeast Harbor, the inn, and the people—Muffy, especially—had already become a part of me.

It was as if I had always belonged here, though I knew that wasn't true. It was premature to experience such deep-seated emotions, to sense my inner self had already become part of the place. That night, as I lay there listening to the tranquility of the world outside, I knew the transformation had begun. I wasn't sure what the next day would bring or how I would adapt to this bewildering new life, but one thing was certain: I had already fallen in love with the place, with its beauty, its mystery, and its people, even those I hadn't met yet. For the first time in a long while, I felt a small, unexpected peace settling into my chest, as though I were exactly where I needed to be.

CHAPTER 8

The First "Real" Day

I woke to a cold May morning, the kind Maine knows well, that sharpness in the air biting your skin. The sea smoke clung to the harbor, a veil of mist that swallowed everything in its path, hiding the water and the boats as if the world were suspended between two realities. Then, gradually, the first rays of the sun broke through, tentative at first, as if unsure whether it had permission to dispel the sea smoke. In that moment, the harbor revealed itself.

The smoke lifted, and there it was—the water, glimmering like a sheet of glass, its surface reflecting the sun's gilded fingers, the world waking up around me in breathtaking beauty. I couldn't refrain from standing for a moment, simply absorbing it all—the cool, fresh air; the ambrosial essence of salt and earth; the beauty of nature so pure and untouched. As if the world had been holding its breath, waiting for me to open my eyes, to see it all.

I felt it in my chest, this pounding beat, this pulse of excitement. Today. Today was my first day at work. The morning felt like a promise, something suspended between hope and the unknown. My emotions raced with anticipation, with a little fear too. I was uncertain, but I was convinced of one thing: the world I had walked into was real. This wasn't a dream. The sun had finally broken through the smoke, and I was here.

I was assigned to the dining room, and as I dressed in the formal uniform—a crisp button-up tuxedo shirt, cufflinks gleaming, a bow tie that felt both too tight and oddly reassuring—I thought of Eugene and Natalia. They were off to housekeeping, their roles already set in stone. But me? I was all alone, about to meet a whole new set of people, ready to confront my first obstacle in this unfamiliar world. I couldn't shake the feeling of being an outsider, even in my own skin. It wasn't only the uniform, which felt like a costume I wasn't sure I could wear, but the sense of stepping into a world I'd never known. The dining room? That was another universe entirely. I had no idea what I was doing. My first shift was dinner service in a fine dining room that felt more like a palace than a restaurant.

The restaurant boasted expensive menus, an intricate wine list I couldn't understand, immaculate table settings where everything had its place, and fresh flowers that breathed life into the space. I was terrified, in a way that only new beginnings can make you. I was expected to "shadow" Colvin.

He had been here for five years, an H2B worker from Jamaica. Colvin was a legend, or so I heard. He moved through the room with such grace, like he was gliding instead of walking, making everything look effortless. I watched him in awe as he approached each table, poised and composed, describing specials with an ease I couldn't imagine. He prepared each table with such care, performing a ritual, each movement precise. The way he spoke, though, I didn't catch every word. His accent, thick and musical, flowed like a river of syllables, and I found myself struggling to make sense of it. He saw the confusion in my eyes.

"Don't worry. You'll get it," he said, his voice warm, reassuring, though there was a hint of impatience. His eyes, though, were kind, and I felt a little relief in that.

I nodded, unsure what else to say. I had no idea what I was doing, but I wanted to. I wanted to be good at this. The hours stretched on, and the rhythm of the evening service grew louder in my ears. The kitchen—a cacophony of noise, chaos, and urgency—was a downright contrast to the peaceful elegance of the dining room. The sound of frying pans clattering, knives chopping, the hiss of the sauté pans, and the rhythmic orders barked by the chefs came together in a rush of tension and energy.

The kitchen felt like a pressure cooker; the heat, the noise, the pace—it was enough to make anyone crack—but there was something captivating about it, something that called to me, as if I could somehow find meaning in the madness. I had never seen anything like it before. The way the chefs moved—shifting between stations, calling orders, adjusting temperatures—it was a dance, a battle fought over the grill, the pass, the garde manger.

I watched in awe as the students from the New England Culinary Institute struggled with timing, trying to get everything right. There was shouting, but not simply anger—frustration, too, the kind that only comes on the verge of breaking. A chef screamed as the once-delicate fish, now overcooked and dry on the edges, lost its texture. I saw steaks cooked to the wrong temperature and sent back. The tension in the air was palpable. The kitchen was both a place of creation and destruction, a balance between mastery and chaos.

Then, there were the dishwashers—the unsung heroes of it all. They moved in and out of chaos, never stopping, never complaining. The clatter of dishes, the scrub of brushes, and the murmur of the washing machine formed their melody, a steady beat that held everything together. I came to realize that without them, none of this would work. The plates, the silverware, the glasses—everything had to be spotless, pristine, and organized. I had once thought of a dishwasher as a menial role, but as I spent more time in the kitchen, I saw the job for what it was: the backbone of the restaurant. Without them, the beauty of the dining room collapsed.

There was a truth in their work that no one else saw. Some of the dishwashers had been coming back every year from Jamaica, a steady presence in the middle of turnover. They were a team, working seamlessly together, each with their own beat, each with their own style, but what struck me the most was the way they cared for each other, the way they made the kitchen a place where joy and work coexisted. They sang to each other, their voices rising over the vibration of the machines, and occasionally, they broke into dance, their movements released from the demands of the work. They had a ritual, each of them—a rhythm in how they washed, cleaned, and organized. I admired them, the way they carried themselves with such grace in the face of the hardest work. No one understood their value, but I did. Without the dishwashers, without the kitchen crew, the whole place crumbled.

I began to work with them, picking up shifts behind the dishwashing machine, learning the importance of their work. I came to realize that unless you had been in the dish pit, unless you had stood there with soap-covered hands, plates piled up around you, you had no right to be in the dining room, no right to call yourself part of the restaurant world. You had to earn your place to be in the front!

The dining room was a thing of beauty. The walls were covered in hand-painted wallpaper, the colors soft yellow and green, dotted with exotic birds and vivid flowers that sprang to life with every glance. The tables, covered in pristine white tablecloths, reflected the glow of the chandelier, their crisp fabric a balance in the warm, inviting atmosphere of the room. The wooden Victorian-style chairs, polished to a gleaming shine, seemed almost too perfect, too elegant for the guests who would soon fill the room.

Despite the formality, there was something warm about it, something charming. The room held a grace that felt timeless, a balance of old-world elegance and modern comfort. The large windows stretched across the entire dining room, offering an unobstructed view of the harbor, the water shimmering in the light as the sun dipped lower in the sky. The fresh flowers on each table mirrored the natural beauty of the world outside, their colors vibrant against the soft colors of the wallpaper. It was as if you were sitting in a garden, surrounded by birds and blooms, the harbor a tranquil backdrop to the muted drone of conversation.

I stood in awe of it all. The space felt alive, a painting come to life, every detail considered, every choice deliberate. It was a place where the ordinary became extraordinary, where even the smallest gesture—the placement of a fork, the curve of a wine glass—had meaning. There was perfection in the air, but it wasn't oppressive. It invited you to be part of it, to step in and become part of the cosmos that had been created here.

As I set the tables, I couldn't help feeling overwhelmed. The sheer quantity of forks, knives, and spoons bore the legacy of a millennium of tradition. I had never thought on what fork went where, or which knife was for fish, and which was for steak. Where did the soup spoon go? What side of the plate did the bread-and-butter plate go on? The intricacy of the details made my head spin.

Everyone around me understood it instinctively, as if they had always known the rules of this world. I, by contrast, was fumbling to remember the countless instructions given to me. In that moment, I realized how little I knew, how much I had yet to learn. The pressure was mounting, but I felt my determination growing stronger. I had to get it right. I needed to prove to myself I could master this world, I could belong here.

So, I threw myself into the task—each small movement, each careful placement of silverware a step toward something more, something bigger. Then came the time to assist Colvin in carrying the food trays. I fumbled awkwardly, my hands clumsy and unsure. Colvin, however, moved with such ease, balancing eight plates as if they weighed nothing, gliding through the dining room with the grace of someone who had done this a thousand times before. I struggled even to pick up the tray, my hands shaking with effort. I watched him closely as he worked, learning from every move, every step. He didn't speak much, but when he did, his voice was calm, even when I made a mistake.

"It'll come," he said once, a kind smile in his eyes, as I struggled with my tray. "Don't rush. Breathe."

It felt like a ritual, this service, a dance that had been perfected over years of repetition. Colvin's movements were so fluid, so natural, and I admired him. It was a grace I had yet to understand, but I knew I would learn it. As the evening wore on, I found myself absorbed in the harmony of the dining room, muted conversation, soft clinks of silverware, and laughter filling the air. Outside, the sun set, casting a warm glow over the harbor. The guests on the patio were relaxed, enjoying the beauty of the evening, sipping their wine and conversing. Soft lighting illuminated the lounge area beyond the patio, with the built-in bar serving as an inconspicuous hub of activity. The colors of the sunset painted the sky in shades of pink and gold, a magnificent scene that slowed down time.

In those moments, as I moved through the dining room, I felt the gravitas of everything I had yet to learn, but I also felt the gentle pride of being part of something bigger than myself. The world of the kitchen, the dining room, and the dish pit—each of them contributed to this experience. I was starting to find my place in it. In due course, I was becoming part of it all.

So, as the evening wore on, I realized that the world I had stepped in to was one of endless learning, endless discovery. For the first time in a long time, I felt as though I was exactly where I was meant to be.

CHAPTER 9

Reflections and Realities

I lay in bed that night, my body thrumming with the aftereffects of my first day. Exhaustion clung to me, but it was a different fatigue than what I had experienced before. It wasn't the heavy, oppressive kind that settles in your bones after hours of physical labor, but something deeper—a mental and emotional exhaustion from being thrust into a world so foreign to me. A world that I had, until now, only thought of.

The day had been overwhelming in its complexity. The details, all of them, had been like a whirlwind around me: the array of forks and knives, the arrangement of the plates, the glasses with their precise positioning. I was still learning the language of the dining room—how to convey a message with the smallest gestures, how to speak through the orchestrated movements that made up the symphony of service. It wasn't the job that exhausted me but the intensity of the sensory overload—the sounds of glass, the sillage of flowers, the sight of perfectly arranged tables, the murmurs I could not yet fully understand. There was an elegance to it all—the shining silver cutlery, the perfectly folded napkins, the warm glow of the chandelier reflecting off polished hardwood floors. It was overwhelming, but it was beautiful too.

The dining room felt like something out of a dream. A place where every motion, every breath, every action had been rehearsed a million times. An arena where perfection was demanded, where each step was deliberate and precise. Even as I marveled at the beauty of the room, I felt the agonizing jab of my own inadequacy. I was so distant from comprehending the beat of the room, from mastering the delicate dance that made it all work. The waiters glided past me, their movements refined and sure, as if they had been born into this world of immaculate service. The guests, too, belonged there, effortlessly fitting into the opulent surroundings, exuding a calm confidence I had yet to learn. They were untroubled in a world where I was an intruder.

I heard their laughter, and I thought of how the dining room, for all its grandeur, had become an arena of judgment for me. Each move, each misstep, felt like a staring imperfection in the perfect framework of the evening. I yearned to understand the unspoken rules of this place, to move through it with grace, to be one with the pulse that kept everything in motion. But I wasn't there yet.

As I lay in bed that night, I felt something I hadn't expected: a strange sort of contentment. It wasn't about perfection—it was the endeavor, the feeling of being alive, trying to catch up with the world around me. Notwithstanding, I was clumsy, and I had made a thousand mistakes, but something in me felt the pull of this new life. This world of polished silverware, exquisite plates, and the intricate dance of service, all set against the backdrop of the sea and the sound of the waves crashing on the rocks. I had no clue how I was going to make it through the rest of the summer, but I realized one thing: I was eager to try.

That night, I was in a small room tucked away with the others in the staff dormitory. Eugene and Natalia, who worked in housekeeping, were in a different room across the hallway. We hadn't spoken much since dinner, but I heard them occasionally as they recounted their day in whispered voices. The walls were thin, and I often found myself listening to the gentle pace of their words, imagining the exhaustion they felt from their work.

I pictured Eugene, his face flushed from running between floors, making sure everything was in place for the guests. His job was demanding in its own way—always on the move, ensuring no detail went unnoticed. Natalia's work was different. She was assigned to clean the rooms that day, a task that, while essential, seemed so far removed from the dynamic world of dining. I heard their tired voices talking—making beds, replacing towels, and cleaning rooms that were immaculate but not as glamorous as the dining room.

I was fascinated by their lives but also humbled. There was an intimacy in the way they spoke to one another, an understanding forged through their shared experience. I sensed the simplicity of their work, the steady beat that carried them through each day. For them, there were no surprises, no curveballs thrown their way. The tasks were clear, the expectations set. They anticipated what the next moment would bring.

In contrast, for me, every moment in the dining room felt like an improvisation. I was trying to learn how to go with the flow of it all, but it wasn't easy. Every table, every guest, and every movement required careful attention. Even the smallest mistake—a misplaced fork, a forgotten wine glass—echoed in the perfection of the space.

"There's a rhythm to it," Eugene's voice floated through the thin walls, and I found myself listening intently. "Once you get the hang of it, it's easy. It's simply knowing where everything goes."

I smiled at the simplicity of his words. I knew what he meant. There was a rhythm in the dining room too, but it was one that I had yet to learn.

"Knowing which rooms are the hardest," Natalia added, her voice light but with a knowing edge. "Room twelve, for example, is always a mess, even though the guests are supposed to be perfect." She laughed, but there was no bitterness in her tone, only a resigned humor. The work was repetitive, yes, but it wasn't without its own challenges.

I wondered, as I listened to them, if they saw their work in the same way I saw mine. For me, the dining room was exciting and full of possibility. Every guest, every course, and every glass of wine was a new opportunity to learn, to improve, and to become part of something greater. For Eugene and Natalia, it was something different: it was a steady, reliable tempo that helped the hotel function—a structure that allowed the rest of us to perform our roles with the precision we needed. Without them, the rest of us had nothing to work with.

They didn't seem to have the same fire for their work as I did for mine. Maybe it was because they were doing it together, or maybe it was because they had seen the quieter beauty in what they did. I admired them, even though our lives were so different. They seemed comfortable with their roles, even if they didn't carry the same glamour as the dining room staff. There was grace in their simplicity, in their subdued ability to get things done without needing recognition for it. I knew that, despite our differences, their work was no less important than mine. It was essential to the smooth running of the hotel.

There was something in the tempo of the dining room, the artistry of the service, that called to me in a way I didn't yet understand. Still, as I lay there in bed, the two of them talking about the lineup they received—room assignments, cleaning lists, duties—I admired it. They had their tasks, and once they'd completed them, the day was over.

For me, it was never that easy. The second the last plate was cleared in the dining room, there was another set of expectations waiting for me. Breakfast service started before dawn, and Colvin had already mentioned I needed to be back in the dining room by five in the morning. The mere thought of it caused a chill to run down my back. How was I supposed to function on so little sleep? But somehow, I knew I would do it. I had to. The task was too important, the work too demanding. And, of course, I didn't want to fail.

The rest of the evening was spent in restless half-sleep, drifting in and out of awareness as my mind replayed moments from the day—

the gleaming silver cutlery, the perfect arrangement of the bread-and-butter plates, and the buzz of muffled conversation. I thought of the guests, the way they sat in the dining room as though they belonged, as though they had always been there. One couple in particular stuck in my mind. The man had worn bright pink pants adorned with a red lobster pattern, a bold statement of personality in a room full of elegance. His companion, an elegant woman with a soft laugh and a gentle smile, seemed like someone who could be in this world effortlessly, without ever having to prove herself.

The way Colvin greeted them—warm, confident—made it clear they were regulars. The kitchen had prepared an amuse-bouche for them, delicate and intricate, which I didn't fully understand. The sommelier had arrived, offering them a bottle of wine so expensive and rare it felt like the air changed when the cork was pulled. Everything about their visit felt rehearsed, effortless, like a play performed on a grand stage. It wasn't simply the food; it was the way they were cared for. Every person in that room knew exactly who they were and exactly how to make them feel special. Even in the calm, behind-the-scenes moments, there was care and precision. Colvin spoke to them like old friends, like family, and I wondered who they really were. I was still so new, but it was clear how much status mattered in the dining room. The guests weren't mere visitors; they were people whose names were known, whose preferences were remembered. It wasn't ostensibly service—it was respect.

As I drifted into a restless sleep, the familiar grip of a recurring nightmare took hold. I was in the dining room, frozen in place as everything around me fell apart. I had forgotten to bring a second set of silverware. I had missed a course. I had dropped plates, broken glasses, and each mistake replayed in an endless loop. My heart raced, my palms sweated, and I felt the encumbrance of failure closing in.

In the silence of the room, as the nightmare faded and my breathing steadied, something shifted. I realized I couldn't allow myself to be consumed by fear. The next day would come, and with it, another set of challenges. I would make mistakes—many mistakes, I was sure of it—but I had to keep moving forward. I had to learn. The dream of becoming part of this world—a world that captivated me, that I had fought to enter—was within reach. It was terrifying, but it was exhilarating.

Tomorrow, I will be ready, rise to meet the challenges with a little more knowledge, a little more grace. One day, maybe not too long from now, I would move through the dining room as effortlessly as Colvin did. For now, all I had was this moment—being alive in the middle of it all. That, for now, was enough.

CHAPTER 10

The Rhythm of Service

The span of time, like the soft ebb of the tide against the jagged rocks by the harbor's shore, stretched endlessly as summer deepened, each day a fusing of toil and revelation. The first few weeks were a blur—a tumult of new faces, unfamiliar tasks, and a world so different it threatened to swallow me whole. However, as the days turned into weeks, I saw more than the polished exterior of the Asticou Inn. I saw its essence, its pulse, the understated undercurrent of life that flowed through every plate of food, every meticulously folded napkin, and every whispered exchange between staff and guest.

Fine dining had once seemed like a distant dream, an idea I only imagined. Over time, I discovered that fine dining transcended formalities or flawless performance. The technique of open-handed service, practiced with precision, became second nature. With each repetition, I came to understand its grace and placid elegance. Serving from the correct side—right to the right, left to the left—wasn't merely a formality; it was an essential principle of fine dining. This method ensured that guests' personal space remained undisturbed, preserving the intimacy of the experience. The rule of never reaching across a guest's plate allowed for fluid communication and a seamless dining atmosphere. Service, I realized, was about creating a space where guests felt comfortable, relaxed, and fully immersed in the moment.

This philosophy extended beyond the table, influencing the

way I approached life itself. Through this cadence, I discovered that service was more than a series of steps; it was a conversation. Each movement conveyed a powerful message. The way one carried a tray, the subtle positioning of a glass, the delicate precision of placing a fork beside a plate—it was all a language. I learned that in this world, the art of serving was not merely presenting food or drinks; it was creating an atmosphere, a sense of belonging, a feeling of being cared for.

As I moved through the dining room, gliding between tables, my every action carried the gravitas of intention and respect. As I stood in the dining room one evening, the bustle of dinner service swirling around me, Colvin motioned for me to approach with a bottle of champagne in hand. The air was heavy, yet all of the background faded as I focused on the task at hand.

"This way," Colvin said, his voice calm amid the chaos. "Let's learn another thing."

I glanced down at the bottle, unsure where to begin. There was something nearly sacred in opening a bottle of champagne in fine dining. I had always associated the *pop* with celebration and victory, the hallmark of a skilled hand. However, Colvin's approach was different—it wasn't about the dramatics of the moment. It was about finesse, precision, and understanding.

"Let's take it step by step," Colvin continued, his tone light but deliberate. "You need to respect the bottle."

I nodded, unsure what exactly that meant. As he spoke, I could tell he wasn't simply referring to the physical object in my hand. There was something deeper he was getting at. He gestured for me to wipe the condensation from the bottle, carefully drying it with a cloth.

"If you forget to do this, you risk losing your grip," he explained, the experience of years evident in his every word. "Most importantly, it sets the tone for the entire process."

I carefully wiped the bottle to dry, feeling the cool surface beneath my fingers as I focused. It felt oddly intimate, even before we had started opening it.

"Now, carefully cut the foil," Colvin instructed, handing me a small knife. "Not too recklessly. This step is very important."

I took the knife and slowly cut through the foil, following his lead. The blade slid cleanly around the bottle neck, and I removed the foil, revealing the wire cage holding the cork in place. There was no rush; Colvin was right—every detail counted. I felt the pressure of the bottle already, a reposeful murmur of anticipation that resonated with the melody of the dining room around us.

"Now, next," he said, eyeing me closely, "take the bottle and tilt it at a forty-five-degree angle. Not too much but enough to ease the pressure. Aim it away from your face. You don't want a surprise or accident."

I followed his instructions, holding the bottle with both hands, making sure to point it safely across the room. As the cork stayed firmly in place, I sensed the building tension within the bottle, and I felt the intensity of the moment. This wasn't a performance for the guests—it was something far more subtle.

"Now, the cage," Colvin said, giving me his reassuring smile. "This is where most people go wrong. You untwist it but gently. Don't rush it. No rush at all."

I untwisted the wire cage, feeling the cork shift beneath my fingers. Instead of simply pulling the cork, Colvin's voice cut through my concentration.

"Hold the cork tightly, be patient," he said. "You're letting the bottle do the work now, not you. Give it time. Don't force it."

I held the cork, steadying it with my hand while the bottle's internal pressure slowly eased the cork upward. I felt the subtle release of air as the cork inched free, a soft sigh rather than the dramatic pop I imagined. The quiet hiss of the bottle was a sound I had come to appreciate—a sound that, to me, now symbolized mastery rather than mere spectacle. It wasn't a show for the guests; it was a thoughtful process that elevated the experience itself.

Colvin glanced at me, a faint smile on his lips. "See? The best way is to let the bubbles stay inside the bottle. That's the key. The pop is a show, but it's not the focus. It's about preserving the effervescence, making sure the champagne stays as it should. That's how you offer an experience."

I poured the champagne into a flute, angling the glass exactly as Colvin had shown me, letting the liquid cascade gently down the side to preserve the bubbles. The effervescence caught the light, rising slowly in delicate spirals. In that moment, it wasn't simply serving a drink; it was presenting something special, something that required a docile understanding of both the product and the audience it was intended for. Colvin's eyes were thoughtful, watching me with approval.

"It's not simply the food or the drink," he said quietly. "It's about making sure it's perfect for the person receiving it. You don't simply serve; you care. You create the space for someone to enjoy every last drop, every moment."

I stood looking at the perfectly poured glass, the bubbles rising gently like the breath of the room itself. I didn't simply see a bottle of champagne anymore—I saw the care, the patience, the harmony of service that made it all come together.

The Asticou Inn was not only for delicate refinement and formal dinners; it was a place of transformation, where ordinary moments were imbued with extraordinary meaning. The lobster bake tours that arrived three times a week were one such example. These events, though far removed from the elegance of the dining room, held their own captivating beauty.

The routine of setting up long, checkered tables covered in bibs and shells seemed absurd in its simplicity. Yet, there was a rawness to it, a conspicuous energy that surged through the dining room as we prepared to serve hundreds of guests, all eager to indulge in the freshest lobster. The process was demanding—an exhausting marathon that left no room for error. The kitchen bustled with activity as the lobsters were boiled alive, their shells snapping with a sinister sound as they plunged into the bubbling water.

(I can still recall the unsettling noise, the desperate, muted cries of the lobsters as they succumbed to the heat. It was a sound that reverberated through the walls of the inn, a reminder of the delicate balance between life and death, between creation and destruction. Yet, it was also a part of the inherent flow of things—one I had come to accept, though never without a certain repugnance deep within me. It was simply a part of the dance.)

As I assisted guests, breaking down their lobsters with a speed that surprised even myself, I found solace in the ritual. The core act of serving became an intimate exchange, a bridge between the rawness of the food and the guests' enjoyment. As my English improved—still rough but now with a bit more confidence—I practiced the lobster instructional speech, delivering it with growing ease, my accent smoothing out with every repetition.

The guests, always curious, asked about my origins, and I eagerly told them of my Russian roots, of the journey that brought me to that moment, in this peculiar yet somehow beautiful world. The stories flowed naturally, the words falling from my mouth with the same ease as I demonstrated how to break apart the lobsters, my hands moving deftly, gracefully, as though the very craft of serving had become a part of me.

It was also during these chaotic lobster bakes when I started to appreciate the nuances of the service—how to navigate between the tumult of the kitchen and the calm of the dining room. Despite the madness that surrounded us, there was something irresistibly satisfying in the work, the way we came together as a team to feed over 150 guests, each one expecting perfection.

Muffy, with her ever-watchful eyes and kind demeanor, was always present during these events, her laughter filling the space as she moved around the dining room, refreshing the flowers and ensuring that every element, regardless how small, was attended to. Muffy's presence was a calming anchor amid the storm, and it was in these occurrences when I saw the depth of her care for the inn and its guests.

She was also the shepherd during the special events—the weddings and rehearsal dinners that perforated the beat of the summer. During these events, the inn exuberantly came to life, and every detail held significance. It was the feeling that permeated the space, the sense of celebration, of connection that made these events so special. Each wedding was a unique affair, united by a shared joy and anticipation. I stood beside Muffy as she meticulously arranged the flowers, each bloom placed with gentle care, each centerpiece a masterful creation. Her attention to detail was unparalleled, and I was mesmerized by the way she awakened life in every corner of the inn. It was then that I felt most connected to her, like a child learning at the feet of a parent.

As the wedding day approached, Muffy oversaw every detail—ensuring the tables were set to perfection, the place cards were alphabetized with precision, chairs were aligned at each table, votives were ready to be lit, and staff uniforms were impeccable. She was always the last to leave the room, ensuring every detail was attended to before the event commenced. It was her, after all the vows had been exchanged, who scrupulously cut the wedding cake, her hands steady and graceful as she sliced into the delicate layers, her eyes shimmering with quiet glee.

By the end of that first summer, I had become her trusted sidekick, at attention beside her as she cut the cake, watching as the guests rejoiced in the sweetness of the moment. There was excitement in that deed, a sense of completion, as though everything had come full circle. In those moments, I began to understand the true meaning of service—not as a duty, but as a calling.

• NEW LIFE, A NEW MENU •

At weddings, at lobster bakes, in quiet instances between the chaos, I learned what it meant to genuinely care for others, to create an experience that transcended the ordinary. The craft of service was not only in food or drink; it created a feeling, making someone's day a little brighter, a little more beautiful. It was weaving together the threads of tradition, skill, and care and offering it to the guests as a gift.

The English-style service, or Silver Service, which Muffy patiently taught me, was the embodiment of this philosophy. In this style, the server presented the food to the guests from a platter with utmost precision and grace. It required not simply skill but deep understanding of timing and of communication between server and kitchen. Each movement had to be deliberate; each gesture carefully executed. It was a form of art, a ballet of sorts, where the server and the guest were partners in a delicate dance. Muffy had shown me the value of this service, how it required emotional intelligence—a compassionate understanding of the needs and desires of the guest. It was not only placing a dish before someone; it was offering them an experience, making them feel as though they were the center of the world, even if only for a brief moment.

So, as the summer drew to a close, I found myself reflecting on the journey I had undertaken—the challenges faced, the lessons learned, and the people who had shaped me along the way. The Asticou Inn was more than a place of work; it had become a home away from home, a place where I discovered the way of life. Muffy taught me more than the intricacies of flower arrangements and the delicate art of cake cutting; she had taught me the virtue of kindness, of diligence, of the subtle power of service. In turn, I had learned to appreciate the complexity of this world—the beauty that lay in the tender gestures, the deepest truths that could be found in the most mundane of tasks.

As I stood beside Muffy, watching the final pieces of a wedding cake disappear, I knew that I was part of something greater than myself—something that transcended the ordinary:

Service is about intention, about being present, about offering something of yourself to those around you.

CHAPTER 11

Between Two Worlds

The lilt of Muffy's car was constant, familiar, a part of my life for the past few months. As we made our way to the Greyhound station in Bangor, the crisp autumn air drifted through the open window, mingling with the subtle unease in my chest. It was not only the physical distance between us and the inn that stretched; it was the distance between the person I was now and the person I had been when I first arrived. It was a reticent transformation, one I felt deep inside, just as the world around changed with the season. The once-green leaves were now suffused with hues of gold and amber, fluttering down in their final dance before they fell to the ground, surrendering themselves to the earth.

Muffy, her hands steady on the wheel, seemed as if she knew exactly what unfolded within me. She had become something of a surrogate mother, someone who shaped my journey in this country, even as I tried to shape my own path. I looked at her briefly, and her face was calm, though I sensed the undertow of emotions she tried to contain. She caught my gaze in the rearview mirror, and for a brief moment, words weren't necessary. We had spent the summer together, side by side, working and learning, and we both knew saying goodbye wasn't as simple as it seemed. There was much hidden beneath the surface, much that lingered in the silence of that juncture.

"I will see you soon," she whispered as we reached the bus station, her words carrying with them an oath of reunion. It wasn't simply a casual phrase—it was a statement steeped in the reality of how our lives intertwined.

As I stepped out of the car and into the brisk air, I felt tightness in my chest. We were parting, but there was no finality to it. At least, not for me. I carried with me the essence of the past months—everything I learned, everything I had become.

The three of us—Eugene, Natalia, and I—boarded the bus to Niagara Falls, a detectable sense of anticipation hanging in the atmosphere. The trip down from Maine to New York State unraveled before me, the colors of autumn increasingly vibrant as we traveled south. The trees had donned their autumn garb, shades of amber and russet blazing against the gray sky. The air had taken on that inimitable, crisp quality—the kind that carries the scent of the earth as it prepares to rest. I thought of how much had changed since I arrived, how much I had changed, and how this season of transformation mirrored my own.

As we drew closer to Niagara Falls, the sheer magnitude of the roaring giant was overwhelming. The growl of the falls reached us long before we saw them, as though mother nature herself called us to witness her power. The Maid of the Mist boat ride took us a hair's breadth from the falls, where the ferocity of the water consumed everything, leaving us soaked, laughing, and spellbound by the beauty before us. It was a gratifying experience, standing amid such grandeur, and I found myself pondering how small I felt when I arrived in this country, but now, confidence and groundedness had taken root in me over the past several months. I was no longer a stranger to this land. I had earned my place here, and the world seemed vast, more open, than it had when I had first set foot on American soil.

We left Niagara Falls behind, heading for the Big Apple, the place that once seemed so daunting. When I last spent time in New York

City, I was a visitor in the truest sense of the word—lost in the maze of streets, overwhelmed by the rush of life that never slowed. Now I was no longer intimidated by the opulence of the city. In merely a few months, my perceptions had changed entirely.

New York had transformed from a monstrous, alien entity to a place pulsating with energy and life where I experienced a sense of belonging. Walking through the streets of Manhattan, I marveled at the urban towers surrounding me. The glass-and-steel facades of the skyscrapers reflected the afternoon sun, casting distinct shadows across the sidewalks. The city was a living, breathing organism, its energy reverberating through the air, in every corner, every building, every person. It was impossible not to be swept up in it, to feel the music of the streets under my feet.

The air was different from what I experienced in Maine—denser, heavy with the scents of food, the tang of exhaust, and the sweet undertones of a thousand different perfumes from the flower vendors lining the streets. The city's fragrances were intoxicating … pizza, freshly baked pastries, coffee, pretzels, and hot dogs. Every corner held something new to discover—something to delight in.

Central Park was a refuge in the middle of it all. We puttered through its paths, the colors of autumn around us so vivid they seemed unreal. The leaves had turned, the trees now wearing their crimson, amber, and yellow cloaks, swaying gently in the breeze. The scent of fallen leaves mingled with the brisk bite of the air, creating an aroma of transition, change, growth. It felt as though the entire world reflected this same process of transformation. In that moment, I reflected again on how I, too, was in a season of transition.

The summer had been one of growth, of self-discovery. As I stood in Central Park, surrounded by the glory of autumn, I knew I was not the same person from months ago. I was someone new, someone ready to tackle whatever came next.

In the Metropolitan Museum of Art, we lost ourselves in the tapestries of history and culture. The paintings, with their vivid colors and intricate details, spoke directly to me. I found myself drawn to a particular painting of a forest in autumn—the trees heavy with ripe fruit, their leaves shimmering in the light of the setting sun. I stood there for a long time, taking in the depth of the palette, the brushstroke textures, and the feeling of warmth that the piece evoked. It reminded me of the moment I was living in—of the way the world was shifting and changing exactly as I was.

Our final night in New York was filled with energy and excitement, a whirlwind of laughter and dancing as we celebrated the closing of one chapter and the beginning of another. We explored Greenwich Village, moving through its vibrant streets, reveling in freedom and possibilities. The lights of Times Square flashed around us, casting long shadows and bathing us in their glow. It was a celebration not only of the city, but of everything that led me here. The late-night cafés, the people, the urban pulse—it all felt like a reflection of my own journey, one that began in the corners of the inn and led me to this precise moment.

As the day ended and we packed our bags in preparation for the return, I took one final inhale of the New York air. There was something about it—the energy, the beat—that I would carry with me long after I left. It was a part of me now, as much as my experiences at the inn. I knew the city would always be there.

We headed to Newark, the bus ride serene as I reflected on the journey that brought me to this point. The world outside the window seemed never-ending, full of possibilities. I made a promise to myself during those sleepless summer nights—that I would continue to push forward, to improve, to grow. I would continue to learn English, take restaurant courses, and prepare myself for the future. For now, I could rest, knowing I had made the most of the opportunities I had been given.

As we boarded the plane and I took my seat, I looked out the window one last time, watching as New York faded in the distance. The sky stretched out before me, vast and infinite, full of promise. The road ahead was long, but it was mine to walk, and I was ready.

CHAPTER 12

Roots and Wings

I stepped down from the train car onto the familiar platform of the Kaliningrad station, and the cool, fall Baltic air immediately filled my lungs. It was saturated with the scent of wet leaves and earth, a fragrance so deeply familiar it feels like coming home. My mom and grandma thrust themselves to my side, their arms enveloping me in endearment and affection. Their hugs were a song for my soul, a gentle reassurance that I was back where a part of me had never left.

My heart swelled, filled with something deeper than gratitude—something more primal. The breeze here, the Russian voices, the sounds of the city—it's all part of me, as if this place has been waiting for me to return, patiently, all this time. I missed them both so much—more than I imagined. I missed the smell of Russian air, that earthy, heavy scent of the city mixed with the filling of autumn. It's not the same as the sharp, cold bite of New York's wind or the thick humidity of Maine's summer mornings. Russian air smells different—more grounding, like stepping back into the embrace of something ancient, something constant.

The sound of the Russian language is music to my ears—the sharp cadence of my mother tongue, the melody of my people, filling me up in a way I didn't realize I needed. The moment feels like a tender reconciliation, a return to something always within me but out of reach for too long. The smell of the city, the familiar sights of the streets, the soft rustling of fallen leaves underfoot—everything felt like a piece of me settling back into place. My roots sank deeper into the ground with every step I took on this land, and yet, part of me still lingered in the other world I left behind. My dad and brother stepped forward, bestowing me with a bouquet of flowers—roses, tulips, chrysanthemums, their radiant colors adding a burst of life to the muted city hues. The gesture was so uniquely Russian, rooted in tradition, and I beamed with pride. It's customary in Russia to greet someone with flowers when they return from a long trip, and this simple gesture felt like an unspoken welcome—a return to something familiar, a marker of tenderness and homecoming.

As we drove through the streets toward my mom's apartment, I watched the city pass by, feeling both a deep sense of peace and a quiet tug of sorrow. The streets were bustling, but there was a sense of calm beneath it all—no rushing, no frantic pace, as if the city itself moved with its own melody, a steady pulse that kept it grounded. It was different from the sprawling chaos of New York, where everything felt urgent, demanding, pulling in all directions. Yet, there was something in Russia's pace that felt more tethered, more certain—there's comfort in that certainty, a feeling of belonging that wrapped around me like a familiar blanket.

Even as I took in the sights—the copper leaves of the trees, the soft light of the setting sun—I can't ignore the other part of me that remains behind in Maine. I think of the gentle mornings by the sea, of the forests that stretched endlessly, of the vast sky above Cadillac Mountain, where everything seemed possible, where I felt like I could breathe in a way I never could here. Maine had become a second home to me, a place that transcended my personal boundaries and I felt the kind of freedom I didn't know I sought. There, time moved slower, and the quiet of the woods had become my companion, filling me up with a sense of possibility, of something new and unexplored. Here, though, I felt the gravity of my past, the grounding vigor of my homeland calling me back. Russia pulled me in with its history, its soul, its weight. Yet, the other side of me—the part that embraced the stillness and the opportunities of Maine—felt like it was slipping away.

How do I reconcile these two parts of me, both so vital, so important?

My mind raced with questions. I was torn between these two worlds, each offering something the other cannot.

As we neared the apartment, a sense of exhaustion fell over me, but it was a weariness filled with both endings and beginnings. I was home, yes, and yet my consciousness pulsated with the awareness that home was more than a singular location. It was the sum of everything I had experienced—both the roots that anchored me and the wings that pulled me toward new horizons. The duality of it all pressed on me, heavy and real. For now, as I entered the calm space of my mom's apartment, I found a strange peace in knowing that, despite the pull of two worlds, this moment felt like a return to something solid, something real. In this moment, I chose to ground myself there, even as the world ahead called me forward.

***

The next college year, I focused solely on improving my English, immersing myself in restaurant operations, and deepening my understanding of service. Every lesson, textbook reading, and hour spent in class became a stepping stone toward mastering not only the mechanics of hotel management but also its inner beauty. I poured myself into my studies, meticulously diagramming table settings and compiling a small notebook that became my most cherished companion for years to come. Each utensil, each glass, each technique—details of the art of service—were etched into my memory. I noted recipes for mother sauces, the intricacies of kitchen operations, and the delicate balance of flavors and presentation. I carried that notebook everywhere, its pages a map to the world I was determined to enter.

It wasn't only about academic achievement. It was about preparation—preparing myself for the next summer adventure, to return to the Asticou Inn and prove not only what I had learned but also the person I had become. I often thought of my time there, watching the chef make hollandaise sauce in the tranquility of the early morning, observing the bartender craft classics like the Old Fashioned, the dry martini, and the Negroni. I marveled at the elegance of decanting wine or opening champagne—each step a ritual, each gesture a language of its own. I longed to understand not merely the process but the passion behind it.

As the winter months passed in a haze of anticipation, my excitement grew. It was not simply the idea of returning to the Asticou Inn that filled me with exhilaration—it was the people who joined me on this journey. Svetlana, a friend I met through classes, had become a constant presence in my life. Her grace, her effortless style, and the way people gravitated toward her fascinated me. She was the type of person who didn't need to try; her warmth, her authenticity, drew people in like the tide. In a world full of noise, Svetlana was a peaceful catalyst, the embodiment of gentleness and strength. She served as my confidante, my reflection, and together, we made plans for our shared future. We were the perfect mismatch—Svetlana with her graceful, understated presence, and me, with my ambition burning a bit too brightly sometimes.

Then there was Roman. Roman, who had become like a brother to me, was my emotional barometer. He had an incredible ability to inspire and ground me in equal measure. In his company, I found both challenge and comfort. His towering presence, warm personality, and unwavering determination made him someone I admired. Roman had grown up with his mother and grandmother, and it showed in the way he was deeply attentive to the needs of those he cared about. But he also believed in pushing boundaries—in challenging me to go further, to reach higher. I often found myself inspired by his drive but also conflicted, knowing that his ambition was at times different from mine, shaped by a desire to prove something I hadn't fully grasped yet.

I came to think of him as my cousin, my close ally in the whirlwind of life. Our trips to the Baltic shore were always filled with magic—each journey marked by laughter, music, and grand plans for the future. He had visited the USA the summer before, and it was there, working at a historic hotel in Pennsylvania, that he too, discovered his affinity for this business. Unsurprisingly, the adventure we were embarking on drew him in, strengthening our bond even further.

Then there was Eugene, our D'Artagnan, the fourth musketeer in our group. Eugene's energy, vigor for life, and loyalty made him an irreplaceable part of our dynamic quartet. Together, we were an ambitious, curious, and fearless group of friends, determined to chase our dreams and learn everything we could along the way. We were on the verge of something truly impactful, something that promised to change us all.

I was ready for the future, for the adventure that awaited us. Yet, beneath the excitement, something always lingered, a subtle undercurrent of sadness, a sense of duality that I couldn't escape. As much as I was looking forward to the next adventure, there was also a deep, raw, nagging ache in my chest. The thought of leaving my family behind, of saying goodbye to the familiar routine of my life in Kaliningrad, weighed heavily on me. I knew I was entering a new phase, and the familiar would fade into the distance, but the idea of not being there for my grandma in her golden years filled me with guilt and sorrow.

It was spring in Kaliningrad—the season I always adored. As the first hints of sun warmed the earth, the city stretched, shaking off the remnants of the cold, dark months of winter. The air was rejuvenating, fresh with the promise of change. It was as if nature had been holding its breath, and now, with a huge sigh, was breathing again. The sky, once heavy with the battened masses of winter, cleared with remarkable speed. The percentage of days shrouded in overcast skies decreased hastily, and the city breathed easier under its warm blue canopy. The tree buds, fragile and delicate, bloomed into vibrant bursts of green and white, metamorphosing the once-barren streets into a kaleidoscope of life.

Spring in Kaliningrad unfolded like an enchanted dream. Along the streets, flower beds erupted in color, as though the ground had given birth to a thousand new lives. There was a balance between the cold lingering in the air and the warmth creeping in. The days, still cool, stretched longer and longer, like the mother earth itself was waking up from a long slumber. I loved the way the days grew longer with each passing week—imperceptibly at first, but as the season wore on, the sky stretched itself out in ways that felt magical. The increasing daylight filled the city with an undeniable energy. I remember the anticipation as I watched the light spill over Kaliningrad's streets, how the mornings lasted longer, and the nights arrived with a gentle warmth, perfect for late walks in the park or drives along the coast.

By late May, the long, golden hours felt like a gift, an endless stretch of possibility. Heading toward the coast, where the water met the land in a dance of light and sound, was the most exhilarating experience of the spring. The Baltic Sea spread out, its vastness both humbling and thrilling. The landscape was lush and green, the shores dotted with wildflowers, their colors vivid against the sky's soft blue. The scent of salt water mixed with the fresh smell of pine, and the sound of the waves crashing against the shore matched the rhythm of my being. The light shimmered off the surface of the water, as if the very ocean were alive with the energy of spring.

Driving along the shore, I could see the vast stretch of the Vistula Lagoon, the water calm and serene, its surface reflecting clear blue. The shores were lined with green, the trees standing tall, branches swaying gently in the breeze. As we passed small fishing villages, simple homes nestled against the backdrop of the forest. The stillness of the place was broken only by the occasional call of a seagull or the whine of our car. It felt like I was in a different world—one both ancient and new, timeless, and fleeting. The pulchritude of the Baltic shore was something that words hardly capture. It was the endless horizon, the brooding waves, and the soft rustling of the trees as they danced in the spring breeze. The natural world imparted the sense it had existed for centuries, unchanged and eternal, and yet, in this flicker, it pulsed with the energy of something new, something exciting.

As we drove, my feelings lingered. There was the pull of this place, this home, where the earth had a soul and my roots felt grounded, and there was the pull of the future that beckoned from beyond the horizon. Kaliningrad, familiar, was my foundation, my ancestry. The world beyond, with promises of new experiences, new friendships, and new adventures, called to me in a voice I simply couldn't ignore. I took a deep breath, feeling the cool air fill my chest, and for a moment, everything seemed clear. I was standing at the crossroads, torn between the soulfulness of my past and the allure of my future. Yet, somewhere deep inside, I fathomed that the journey ahead brought me closer to myself, regardless of where I went.

CHAPTER 13

The Great Return

The car's tires crunched over the gravel as it rolled to a stop, the sound of it cutting through the quiet like a soft exhale, a sigh of release. We had arrived. The Asticou Inn, always inexorable, always familiar, stood right in front of us, but today, there was something different. It was more than the old timbered walls or the vines creeping up the trellis; today, it felt as though the inn itself had been waiting for this exact moment. There was a tangible anticipation in the ether, in such a manner as the world decided to suspend time for us. The sun loitered low in the sky, its warm rays bathing the grounds in soft, gilded light. The flowers, blooming in a pandemonium of tones, painted the landscape with vibrant hues—azaleas in shades of pink, white, and lavender filled the air with beguiling scent, while lilacs in purple and blue sway gently in the breeze. The earth seemed alive, soaking up the warmth, the scent of spring mingling with the sharp tang of fresh leaves. Everything felt new, like a canvas waiting to be filled with reveries.

When the car door opened, I barely had time to think before my feet were carrying me forward, as if the land beneath my shoes called me home. Muffy was there, waiting, as I had known she would be, standing in the soft glow of the afternoon sun, her figure framed by the blossoms around her. The moment our eyes met, time stretched, then collapsed on itself. Without a second thought, I rushed into her arms. Her citadel was more than a welcome; it was a reunion of souls, a meeting of months and spaces that had seemed to separate us but never really had.

Her laughter came in a rush, like the sudden breaking of a dam, and tears of joy spilled from her eyes, tracing the lines of her face. She didn't need to speak to express how overjoyed she was to see me; the pure jubilee in her embrace, the warmth that radiated from her, said everything.

I introduced Roman and Svetlana, and for a moment, the three of them stood in silence, taking in the scene. Muffy's gaze was sharp but warm, welcoming them without words, a silent understanding passing between them. Eugene, of course, needed no introduction. The instant he stepped forward, Muffy's smile deepened, and in the space of a heartbeat, the months between them dissolved. Her hug, tender and full of unspoken affection, held him as if nothing had ever changed. It was a moment of tranquil perfection, a simple gesture that felt like the unbroken thread of a long friendship.

The air was thick with the perfume of flowers, the scent heavy and sweet, mixing with the crispness of the late spring air. The sky above us stretched endlessly, a deep, clear blue, and the warm sun soaked into my skin, as though it had been waiting all year to greet us this way. The leaves on the trees whispered in the breeze, a soft rustling, as if the earth were sighing in contentment. Across the street, the Azalea Garden was a painter's palette come to life. The flowers painted the landscape in shades of pink and violet, their delicate petals catching the light as if they were made to reflect the beauty of the day. Everywhere I looked, there was color, there was life, and for a moment, it felt like nothing could ever change. The world was whole, perfect, and still.

Beneath this peaceful surface, something stirred in me—a silent ripple of uncertainty. This was the world I left behind, a world unchanged, a world familiar and safe. But this return carried onus, an awareness that what I knew had changed. The world around me had blossomed, yes, but so had I, and the changes in me were not easily ignored. This wasn't simply a return; it was the beginning of something novel. A new chapter in a place I once called home, but now, in the glow of this afternoon, I felt the gap between the person I had been and the one I had become.

The change was subtle but undeniable. There was a hushed excitement pulsing inside me, a flutter in my chest as I navigated the familiar spaces, now layered with expectation. There was infinitely more I wanted to prove this summer, and the stakes felt higher than ever. My English was better; I heard the subtle differences in the language now—the way words could sing and dance when they were used precisely and correctly. Even with this progress, I realized I still had much to learn. I wasn't yet who I wanted to be. I was still a student, grasping at the nuances, trying to make my mark in a world that felt larger and more complex than I imagined.

There were new people now too. People who didn't know me from last summer, who had no preconceptions or expectations. I felt a strange pull to prove myself to them, to show I had grown, to show I had something to offer, even though they would not know the difference. It was as if the stakes of my identity had shifted. No longer was I returning to an acquainted place; I was trying to reinvent myself, to redefine who I was on my own terms. The pressure and preconceived notions? They weighed on me greater than I wanted to admit.

We made our way to the Hilltop, where our new "quarters" awaited. It was a place of possibilities, a blank canvas ready to be painted with whatever colors this summer brought. This time, I would not face it alone. My traveling companion, Svetlana, and Anya, her best friend from high school, shared this chapter of my life. It was a new beginning, a new "episode," but one steeped in everything that came before.

Inside the kitchen, the routine sounds of the world resonated warmly—dishes clattering, faint conversations, and comforting smells of something delicious being prepared. I spotted Colvin first, his broad grin lighting up his face as soon as he noticed me. Before I said a word, he enfolded me in his embrace, and in that moment, the world's gravity lightened. It was the type of hug that belonged to an old friend, one that never needed words to make its meaning clear.

Roman and Svetlana stood inside the doorway, wide-eyed but smiling, eager to step into this world that had become my home away from home. I was eager to show them around, to introduce them to friends who were like family, and to walk them through the warmth and controlled chaos of the kitchen that always felt like mine. Yet, as I moved through the familiar spaces, a strange tension lingered in the back of my mind. This return, this rekindling, did not evoke a sense of closure; it felt like a pause more than anything. A moment arrested in time, a place between inhales. The inn, with its flowers and sunlight, felt too perfect, too pristine, as though it were a stage set to hide things stirring beneath the surface.

Muffy's arms, Colvin's smile, and the laughter in the kitchen—they all offered refuge, a balm to my restless heart. Beneath it all, I felt a subdued storm gathering, waiting close beyond the horizon. Something had shifted inside me. The path ahead, which had once seemed so certain, now seemed blurred and uncertain.

CHAPTER 14

Echoes of Understanding

The evening sun slumbered over the inn, casting a glistening hue on the flower-drenched grounds, as if the world itself were taking a silent breath in preparation for the night ahead. The cold breeze from the harbor kissed my face, a whisper of salt and promise, while I meticulously set the stage for what would surely be an elegant dinner service. I moved around the dining room like a conductor preparing for a symphony—each polished fork, each crystal-clear wine glass, each immaculate menu a note to be played at exactly the right time. The silver gleamed under the soft light, reflecting the sun's fading rays in an ethereal way.

I moved with purpose—this summer, the heft of ambition sat heavily on my shoulders. My position as a server was a building block. I would prove myself, test my mettle, and earn a leadership role in the inn, which promised not simply a paycheck but respect and the opportunity to wield a small amount of power. I took a final sweep of the dining room, mentally checking off each station as ready. The linens were crisp, the water pitchers were filled and waiting, and the candles were just so, flickering in the growing twilight. A few more details to attend to, and then I could relax, maybe grab a breath before the rush of guests tumbled through the doors.

With the dining room set, I ventured to the adjacent deck, the aromas of flowers and salt air filling my lungs. The tables there, too, were prepared—each chair placed precisely, each umbrella elegantly positioned to offer guests shade as the evening sun dipped. As I pulled the last umbrella free, I felt it—a shift in the air. A presence. Not the passing murmur of wind or the idle chatter of the inn staff. Nay, this was an experience of an altogether different nature. Utterly still, utterly calm, like the sudden absence of sound before the clamor of thunder. Someone was watching.

I paused, mid-motion, and turned. There, standing awkwardly near the threshold of the dining room, her hands fidgeting with the edges of her shirt, was a figure I had not yet seen. She stood in the doorway, neither stepping forward nor retreating, simply watching. I had never known her, not yet, but something in the way she stood in the periphery caught me—her uncertainty was like a mirror to my own ambitions, my own sometimes-tenuous footing in this world.

Before the silence stretched longer, Muffy's familiar voice rang out. Her gentle, mischievous tone softened the awkwardness of the moment.

"Meg," Muffy said, stepping into the frame of the door and flashing a smile as inviting as it was disarming, "this is our newest addition. She's the one who's been giving this place that extra touch of brilliance."

Muffy's voice was the opposite of Meg's. Where Muffy embodied warmth, the kind that made you feel immediately at home, Meg's silence held a gravity that made me pause. She was not simply another summer server. No, there was something deeper there, something not immediately detectable—an intrinsic, quiet strength that folded itself neatly into the way she held herself. She wasn't some privileged girl here to spend her summers collecting experiences to be molded into stories of lavish indulgence. She was, like me, here for something far more expedient—because she needed to be here.

Her story unfolded over the course of those first couple days and then the summers that followed. It was an undercurrent of tacit understanding between us, though we never had to articulate it. She had not been born into wealth, had not been trained in the genteel ways of private schools and Ivy League privilege. She was from the working-class neighborhoods of Boston, raised by a mother who wrestled to stay afloat, whose sacrifices were the only luxury Meg had known. It was that exact struggle that forged her—honed her into a person who not only worked hard but worked with purpose.

When we talked late at night, as the white noise of the inn faded into the background and the stars climbed into their places, Meg spoke of her road to this junction—how she decided to change the course of her life. She wasn't some coddled dreamer; she was a person who looked at the world and made a choice: not to be its victim but its mason. She didn't simply want to live; she wanted to shape her existence, chisel a path out of the raw material of her own determination. Her eyes sparkled with something that couldn't be contained in simple words, the same concealed ferocity I recognized in myself but had never seen so eloquently embodied. Where others worked for luxury, for experience, for the sake of fleeting pleasures, Meg's work ethic was driven by something infinitely more substantial: purpose.

And the guests? She *cared*. She cared for each of them as if they were the only ones in the world, as if their joy or frustration was the precise thing that defined her day. There was an utmost earnestness in the way she carried herself, something that didn't simply care but understood, deeply, the fragility of human experience. Perhaps it was that very quality that lured me to her in the first place. Meg wasn't solely another person passing through my life. She became something more—someone. A wayfarer who, over the next two summers, would unravel the core of who I was, challenge my worldview, and ultimately reshape it. Our friendship was not born in the conventional sense, not in the trivial exchanges that characterize most relationships, but in the hard, shared moments that demanded introspection and required real thought—the kind that burns away the surface-level distractions.

That first surely awkward moment? It became a part of the legend we created, the unspoken tale of two fellow wanderers who found each other by pure happenstance, or perhaps by the imperceptible threads of fate that always pulled at the right time. The awkwardness faded, but the alliance we crafted never lost its depth. We became inseparable, two individuals who sought the same thing from life—an opportunity to transcend, to rise above, to prevail. To be more than what the world said we should be. That, in the end, was the foundation of everything that followed.

The summer stretched on, and with it, our friendship solidified, not in one loud moment, but in the reposeful spaces between shifts, the unspoken rituals we grew into. Asticou was alive with the usual summer frenzy—college kids from all over, their laughter ringing through the halls, their carefree revelry and spending habits, a sharp incongruity with Meg and me. We were like outsiders in a world that didn't quite belong to us. While others lived for the party, for the fleeting pleasure of expensive drinks and louder nights, Meg and I found solace in the quiet corners of the world—whether it was behind the bar, grasping the art of drinks from her, or escaping into the wilds, the trails of Acadia becoming our refuge. Though she didn't live at the Hilltop with the others, Meg's presence there became constant, a silent string that laced us closer as the days went by.

After every shift, while the others rushed to the bars or climbed into the back seats of cars to chase the next high, we often stayed behind. It wasn't that we didn't want to profligate; in truth, we both were as capable of enjoying a good drink. Our indulgence was different—it wasn't in the loud, sugary cocktails, the cheap beer, or wasting money. No, our vice was a taste of something we couldn't ordinarily afford—a bottle of leftover wedding wine that the inn kept as if it were some secret treasure. It wasn't much, but it was enough. Sitting with the bottle between us, we'd savor each sip, arguing the notes of the wine as though we were sommeliers at some prestigious establishment. That was our joy—an education in the subtlety of things, a skillful exploration of taste that few ever think to study at the end of the shift with a leftover bottle.

Meg was my teacher in so many ways. Though she was an experienced bartender, always behind the bar at the fanciest events, concocting drinks with an ease I could never master, she never made me feel less than capable. In fact, her patience was a marvel, something I lacked. I was a novice, clumsy with shakers and mixing glasses, but she explained every step, from the simplest cocktail to the most elaborate potions. She was a master of the craft, guiding me through the process, teaching the steps of preparation and presentation, the art of mixology. She was a guide and a mentor, pulling me into her world of bartending, where every ingredient had its place, every garnish its purpose, and every drink its story.

One day, toward the end of summer, Meg and I were bartending an event together, the lounge area of the inn alive with the hum of 120 guests, and the deck spilling out with people eager for the evening's festivities. It was controlled chaos, a dance we knew by instinct. Our movements accorded—pouring, stirring, shaking, passing glasses. Then, without warning, disaster struck. Two built-in shelves of the bar collapsed, sending bottles crashing to the ground. The noise was clamorous, a glass-shattering roar, as bottles tumbled in every direction. For a split moment, there was nothing but silence. The crowd froze.

But Meg and I, you ask? We were already in motion, trying impetuously to catch bottles as they fell, dodging shards of glass and frantic chaos. In the fury of it, we locked eyes—no words spoken, but an understanding passed between us. Without hesitation, we straightened up and turned to the guests.

"We are fine," we said in unison, our smiles unfaltering. "Please, continue to enjoy this beautiful evening."

It was how we worked—together, no matter what, no matter the situation. In those moments, we rose to the challenge, our composure intact. We finished the service smelling like liquor, our faces still bearing smiles so the guests wouldn't feel the magnitude of the incident. When the night ended and the last guest left, we were exhausted but proud of how we had handled it. We laughed as we cleaned up the mess, remembering the surreal moment, the silence. Even in the aftermath, we knew we'd gotten through it because of our connection—our camaraderie. It was another test of our ineffable bond.

Beyond the drinks and the late-night shifts, there was deeper connection in the long, unobtrusive hikes we took each day. With small breaks between shifts, we'd slip away—me, an extrovert desperate to escape the buzz of socializing, and her, the more reserved, aloof presence who preferred solitude. Together, we'd hike from the Asticou to Thuya Garden, sometimes all the way to the summit of Sargent Mountain. The paths of Acadia National Park became our shared sanctuary, the calm refuge from the frenzy of our working lives.

With each step, we grew closer, the land beneath our feet echoing the conversations we'd only begun to have. Meg's humor, caustic and astute, went beyond my grasp for a long while, but when it hit, when I finally understood the depth of her wit, I saw why people found her so different. It was her mind, incisive and unyielding, the kind of humor not everyone could catch. She wasn't always the star of the show, but when she spoke, it was often the most enlightening, the most piercing. I admired that about her.

In a way, Meg and I were opposite. I was outgoing, easily made friends, and lit up rooms without trying. I always felt like I had something to learn from her. She was quieter, more introspective, and didn't need the approval of others to be comfortable. We balanced each other. I helped her navigate those moments when her awkwardness felt too much—too exposed in social settings. She helped me slow down, think before I spoke, and unearth significance in things I usually skimmed over. Our friendship wasn't only in shared interests; it became masterful, learning from each other's strengths, finding comfort in our differences.

NEW LIFE, A NEW MENU

That first summer, I learned more from Meg than I expected. Not only about cocktails and wine, but how to see the world through a lens of subtle understanding. In return, I hope I taught her a bit about stepping into the spotlight, embracing who you are, even when it feels uncomfortable. We became an unlikely duo, and yet, in that odd harmony of opposites, we uncovered something real, something that lasted beyond summer's end.

CHAPTER 15

The Weight of Departure

The train station, with its cold stone platform and its ever-present sounds of departure, was a place of finality. There, beneath the indifferent, gray Kaliningrad sky, the world narrowed into a single painful truth: I was leaving for good. It was the spring of 2003. The rattle of the train grew louder, each screech a reminder of the thousands of miles between me and everything I had ever known. It wasn't only the physical distance that crushed my chest—it was the emotional distance, the expansive rift between my familiar world and the one I was entering. My mother stood there beside me, her fragile figure braced against the wind, her face an unreadable canvas of conflicting emotions. I wanted to speak so badly, to comfort her, to say something deep-seated—but all that came out was a murmur, barely a sound that bridged the gap between us.

The silence between us grew heavy, a thing to be feared, yet it was the only language we both knew in that instant. I was embarking on my third summer at the Asticou—this time, a step that marked my decision to stay, to plant roots, however far from her I went. Her eyes, those eyes that watched me grow from the tiny girl in a florescent jacket to the woman standing before her now, were brimming with something I could not decipher at first. Sadness? Yearning? Yes, but also something significantly more, something deeper—a inconspicuous pride, a reverence I only half-understood at that moment. Her hands trembled as they clutched the fabric of her raincoat, a subconscious movement, as if she were attempting to hold onto something slipping away.

"I'll be fine, Mama," I murmured, but the words felt hollow, ringing against the emptiness of the platform. I was trying to convince myself more than her.

She didn't answer immediately. Instead, her gaze held mine, and for the first time, I vividly saw her the way she had always seen me. The girl who was going to the far-off land to make a life for herself, to build something from nothing. My heart ached for her in ways I could never explain. This wasn't the goodbye of childhood summer break. This was the severing of a tether that had bound us for years, the painful acknowledgment that we were no longer living in parallel worlds but in separate spheres. The dreams I harbored were hers, too, but they had taken a different shape, one that was lived out in the hills of Maine and the realm of the American East Coast.

A sharp breath caught in my chest as I held her gaze. I saw the exact moment when she allowed herself to relinquish me to the world that awaited. It was as if a wave of realization crashed over her—her little girl, the one she nurtured, the one who clung to her side through thick and thin, was now flying into the unknown.

"I'm proud of you," she finally spoke. Her voice, barely above a whisper, cut through the air like a knife, precise and heavy.

There it was—the final, irrevocable approval. A mother's pride, tempered by the unspeakable grief of knowing she was losing her child to something larger than herself.

I only nodded, unable to speak for fear of shattering the delicate stillness of the moment.

The train's horn sounded in the distance, its call echoing in the hollow spaces between us, as though warning us of what was to come—what we both already knew was inevitable. I stepped forward, my bag swinging lightly at my side. As I turned to board, I felt a hand on my shoulder—her fingers, cold against my skin, grounding me one last time. She didn't say anything more, and I didn't look back. We both knew there was nothing more to say. The doors of the train closed behind me with an oppressive finality.

The world started to move, and for a moment, everything paused. I felt the weight of my mother's love and sacrifice pressing against my chest, an overwhelming feeling that stayed with me, even as the train pulled away, carrying me toward the life I had chosen for myself, away from the life I was born into.

So, the next chapter began.

As the years at the Asticou blurred into one another, I moved deeper into a life that had begun to feel, at times, written for someone else. The work—tiring, relentless, yet strangely satisfying—molded me into something I hadn't anticipated. I had become more than a part of the inn; I had become its vital essence.

As I became the dining room manager, each day felt like the next logical step in a progression that was inexorable, yet always surprising in its depth. It wasn't simply the long shifts, the heft of responsibility, or the frantic pace of wedding after wedding—it was how I was learning to belong to the place. It was in these moments, within the delicate routines of polished glasses and perfectly placed silverware, I understood the real nature of service. I had mastered the dance of catering to the whims of strangers, each one expecting something different yet all wanting the same sense of reverence. Even as my responsibilities increased, something gnawed at me. This was, after all, still temporary.

The seasons would change again, and once they did, so, too, would I. The question I found myself asking most often, lying in bed late at night, was, where was the line between this life and the next? Was this a series of stepping stones to something grander, or was this—this work, these people, this space, my life—fully realized? The calm, reflective moments after a busy evening—when the last guests had left, and the only sound was the clinking of glasses—gave me little space to contemplate.

It was on these occasions that Muffy took me aside, sharing with me her wisdom about the true nature of hospitality, people, life itself. Muffy's generosity toward me knew no threshold. At the season's conclusion, Muffy insisted on taking me to some of the finest restaurants in Bar Harbor or Bangor—places where linen-draped tables, crystal chandeliers, and unblemished service were the order of the day. At these dinners she insisted I order whatever my heart desired, no matter the price, no matter the extravagance, something I could never afford on my own.

"Order it!" she would exclaim, a playful twinkle in her eyes, as though her joy at treating me was greater than the act itself, sharing a delicate dessert at Michell's restaurant. A chocolate box filled with mousse and fresh seasonal berries. We smiled at each other, relishing each morsel, our connection deepening in that simple, perfect moment. These dinners, these small gestures of kindness, became a ritual. A moment for me to breathe, to reflect on the work done, to celebrate my survival of another season.

They were also much more—a symbol of the bond Muffy came to represent for me. She had become the mother I left behind. A figure of steady, quiet nurturing, with hands that soothed anxiety and an energy that seemed boundless in its warmth. Her home in Northeast Harbor was my sanctuary on days when the weightiness of everything became too much. It was there, surrounded by the peaceful sound of her cats playing and the murmur of conversation, I felt grounded again. Muffy named one of her cats "Kiska," a name that, to me, was a constant reminder of my roots, even when I felt far from them. She was, perhaps unknowingly, the anchor I needed in the storm of my life. Without her, I may have lost myself in the harshness of trying to prove I could succeed in a place that, though welcoming, was still foreign.

Our drives down Sargent Drive, where we'd gaze out over

the fjords' crystalline waters, became a metaphor for what I was trying to do with my life—navigate uncertainty, guided by Muffy's inconspicuous presence. In her company, I learned the power of simplicity, the beauty in looking at the world as it was, unburdened by relentless pressures of ambition and expectation. When she spoke of old money, well-rooted affluent families whose private dinners we catered, telling me stories of their opulence, their generational wealth, I was reminded of how different life could be for some. Muffy, with her humility, never let that divide us. She always returned the conversation to something grounded—nature, history, or her cats—and for that, I was eternally grateful.

As summers at the Asticou came to an end, I found myself looking ahead, not to the next season, but to something uncertain. The decision to leave for Clearwater, Florida wasn't made lightly. After long days at the inn, where I built not just skills but a reputation, I had grown restless. I recognized the need for a fresh challenge, one that pushed me beyond my limits. Winters at the Asticou were dormant, with the bustle of summer replaced by slow, heavy silence of the offseason. So, after much thought, I decided to make my way to Florida, where Konstantin had invited me to join him in a small Italian restaurant on Clearwater Beach. It wasn't grand or glamorous, but it was new—a departure from everything I knew and a chance to stretch the boundaries of my experience. I would leave in December, after the last of the leaves had fallen from the trees of Acadia and the first snow dusted the streets.

By then, I was entrenched in the life I had built, and the thought of leaving Muffy was difficult. It was a wrenching farewell, filled with both joy and sadness, like the bittersweet taste of wine too fine to be appreciated at the moment. Muffy gave me her blessings with a soft smile, and as I drove away from Northeast Harbor, her face was etched in my mind—a face of strength and gentleness but also of the sorrow that comes with knowing a chapter is closing.

The winter I spent in Clearwater was as transformative as it was humbling. Working in the small, family-owned restaurant—more like a piece of Tuscany than Florida—was different than the refined operations of the Asticou. Authenticity and simplicity reigned, and I learned new things daily: how to make the perfect espresso, how to bake bread from scratch, and how to transform a small, intimate restaurant into something that felt like home to its patrons.

The owners, Fulvia and her husband, were always present, their passion for food evident in every meal. The restaurant was housed in a quaint space, the entrance shaped like a wine barrel, with low ceilings and soft lighting that transported diners to another world. Working alongside Konstantin, I learned a different approach to service—intimate, focused, and personal in its approach. It was simplicity, yet the lessons were vast. With Konstantin and my new friend, Glen, I understood the spirit of genuine service.

Glen, with his unshakeable calm and his near-perfect sense of urgency, taught me more. I struggled with the fast-paced demands, the eighteen daily specials to be memorized and recited at the table, while Glen breezed through them, effortlessly managing both the guests and the floor with a grace I never seemed to achieve. It was in the simplicity of it all—the small restaurant, the unobtrusive companionship of Konstantin and Glen, the slow harmony of the seasons—that I found something deeper within myself. The rush of the Asticou's busy summer days, the stress of managing the dining room, the tangibility of leadership—all of it felt like part of a grander narrative, one pulling me toward a future I did not yet fully see.

So, I spent my winters in Clearwater, a small dot on the map, comprehending new things not merely about service but what it meant to build a life, step by step, brick by brick, and to carry those lessons back with me when the snow melted, and the world was reborn. This is also when I began my adventure with the Innisbrook Resort in Palm Harbor, though marked a chapter of its own, to be told later.

CHAPTER 16

The Glances of Transition

The final day at the Asticou felt like a dream unraveling—disjointed, almost beyond my grasp. The hours blurred, yet each fleeting moment seemed etched in sharp relief, a vivid snapshot that wouldn't fade, not even in the most distant corners of my mind. It was as if the inn, with all its history, its countless stories woven into the fabric of the familiar walls, stood still as I moved through it, somehow suspended between departure and the memories it held. Seven years. It had been seven years since I first walked through those doors—wide-eyed, unsure, hopeful. In the span of seven years, a thousand things can change. Allergies shift. Taste buds evolve. The scent of a place that once seemed foreign becomes familiar, like skin. And a life—my life—can reshape itself entirely, folding and unfolding in ways I never predicted.

I made my way through the dining room for the last time, polished floors beneath my feet reflecting the glow of chandeliers. I heard the echoes of laughter from those long-ago evenings—the guests who had long since become family. Their voices mingled with people from other summers, mild-toned conversations where smiles were exchanged over glasses of wine and the soft jingle of silverware against fine china. These moments of connection were more than fleeting pleasantries; they were the invisible threads that had tied me to this place. The Asticou, in its elegance, had become my home away from home. As I walked through the corridors, I thought how this space had shaped me. It was here, under its low, elegant beams, where I learned what service truly meant—not simply the mechanics, but the soul of it. I acquired the skill of seamlessly transitioning a dining room from one meal to the next, mastering the movement between weddings and dinner service with such precision it felt akin to art. The hurried evenings spent resetting the room, the exhaustion of waking only a few hours after the last guest left to prepare for the first breakfast service—all of it was part of a flow that now, in hindsight, felt timeless.

The Asticou wasn't simply a business; it was a selfless endeavor, for the most part. A privately owned inn, profit wasn't the driving force; it was always preservation, maintaining historical integrity. There was no corporate structure, no quarterly reports. The inn was owned by a group of affluent individuals who spent their summers on the island. The inn, with its unique role in the story of Acadia, represented more than a place to stay—it was a legacy. Their goal was to ensure that this iconic establishment endured for generations, serving as both a symbol of their status and a testament to their commitment to its preservation. That was a lesson ingrained in me over the years. The inn's true wealth wasn't in profits but in its ability to stand the test of time—exactly as I had done, learning and growing in its shadow.

Muffy stood like a pillar in the chaos of the kitchen, a calm vanguard amid the storm of clattering pans and sizzling orders. She was a woman of few words, but in that final moment, as I stood in the doorway watching her work, I realized our connection had been far-reaching. There was no need for words between us. Every glance, every nod, every shared moment of silence had already said everything that needed to be said. Yet, I felt the substance of it—the gravity of this final departure. Her hands moved with practiced ease, the rhythm of her actions a testament to years of hard work, the hours spent in this exact space that shaped not only my understanding of service but my entire professional life.

As I stood there, taking in the last vestiges of this place, it dawned on me I was leaving more than a mere job behind. I was leaving a piece of myself. Seven summers at the Asticou felt like a lifetime. Seven years of weddings, rehearsals, and those grand "Friends of Acadia" events. Each year, the elite of the island came together, their laughter ringing through the air as they dined beneath the great tent by the harbor. The extravagance of it—endless trays of lobster, wine, and the finest delicacies—was not lost on me. The guests sipped champagne, talking of the future of the island, pledging support for its preservation with every toast.

Beyond the spectacle, there was a certain reverence in the way people connected to this land, a deep, unspoken respect for the history of Acadia. It wasn't only the elite who were part of this world. There was the end-of-summer dinner dance, a celebration that felt as much about showmanship as tradition. I remember the guests—dressed in bright colors and quirky patterns, their boat shoes tapping against the floor in sync with the music from a band flown in from New York City. The dance floor was alive, filled with people trying to outdo one another in the most extravagant orders of wine and the most expensive cuts of steak. Yet, beneath it all, there was bliss in the excess, a pleasure in being part of something grand. Those events, those high-stakes nights that required everything to be perfect, taught me what it genuinely meant to serve—to anticipate, to exceed expectations, to create an experience that felt not only seamless but almost divine in its execution.

Leaving the Asticou was not simply walking out of a job—it was stepping away from a place that shaped my being's very marrow. I packed not only uniforms and memories, but a version of myself I spent seven summers becoming. There was no ceremony, no grand farewell. Only the quiet ache of departure, silence between glances, and unspoken knowledge that a chapter was closing. I didn't know what lay ahead—only that it would be different. Different in beat, in scale, in spirit. But I carried the Asticou with me: its lessons, its elegance, its grace under pressure. From the harbors of Maine to the palms of Florida. From intimacy to infrastructure. From preservation to precision. The road to Innisbrook began not with ambition, but with reverence—for what I had lived, and what I was becoming.

So, I moved to Florida full time, carrying both gratitude and gravity. The transition felt less like a leap and more like a quiet crossing—one marked not by certainty, but by resolve. I didn't arrive with a grand plan, only the intention to keep moving forward, to stay open to what the next place might teach me. The season ahead was unknown, but I trusted the foundation I had built would guide me wherever I landed.

I returned to Innisbrook, where I had worked part-time during the winters prior to this move, now ready to step into something more.

At Innisbrook, I quickly realized the importance of efficiency in an environment where every second counted. I began analyzing workflows—how we moved between tasks, the timing of orders, and the communication flow between the front and back of the house. I worked with the team to optimize these processes, cutting down unnecessary steps while ensuring the service level remained exceptional. In many ways, it felt like learning a new language, where every decision had ripple effects throughout the operation.

When I left the Asticou, heading toward Innisbrook, I felt the heft of the transition pressing down on me. It was a shift not only in geography but in the essence of the work I did. Innisbrook was vastly different from the intimate, hands-on environment of the Asticou; it was part of a corporate landscape, a world of Standard Operating Procedures and financial statements. I once thought my time at the inn had prepared me for anything, but when I walked into Innisbrook, I realized how little I truly knew.

The resort itself was stunning—a sprawling complex of golf courses, lush greenery, and towering oaks that offered a serene sense of peace in the axis of Palm Harbor, Florida. Yet it was different from Acadia. The island's rugged cliffs and sweeping vistas had been a constant presence in my life. Florida, by comparison, felt flat; its landscape was vast in its own way but not as immediate or tangible as the forested hills. Still, there was something in the tranquility of Innisbrook that made me feel like I had stepped into a new chapter.

Here, amid the luxury of Salamander Hotels' takeover, I fully grappled with what leadership meant. At Innisbrook, I took on the role of restaurant manager at the steakhouse—an establishment I worked at several winters before—but now, I was stepping into a different capacity, tasked with leading a team of seasoned professionals. I had to navigate the intricacies of service and the complexities of corporate culture. It was a sharp contrast to the laid-back, family-like environment at the Asticou, where we all knew each other, where each guest was treated like an old friend. At Innisbrook, I found myself surrounded by seasoned staff, each with their own expectations, accustomed to the rigid standards of corporate operation. I was no longer a part of the team; I was expected to lead, to shape the environment, and to ensure every guest had the experience they had come to expect.

I met Hayato, a man whose discipline and relentless pursuit of perfection were unlike anything I had ever experienced. His approach to service was unwavering, his expectations high, and his standards nonnegotiable. He didn't want results; he demanded excellence.

"Do you want to be small fish in a small pond?" he asked me, his gaze steady, unwavering, "or large fish in a large pond?"

In that moment, I understood the true onus of what I had stepped into. The stakes were higher now, and I would have to grow in ways I had not anticipated.

With Hayato's guidance, I learned that leadership wasn't delegating tasks. It was about vision, understanding the needs of your team, fostering an environment where excellence was the baseline, not the exception. He pushed me, forcing me to see beyond the surface, question my assumptions, and demand more from myself and those around me. His Japanese heritage, with its deep-rooted discipline and respect, became the lens through which I viewed my own role as a leader.

At this precipice, I reflected on everything that brought me to this moment. The beauty of Acadia, the lessons learned at the Asticou, the buzz of the electric buses that carried me through those summers, and the faces of guests who shared their stories with me—each memory was now part of who I had become. They were the foundation upon which the next chapter would be built. Yet, despite the vastness of the road ahead—despite the corporate world I was now part of—I felt an odd sense of peace. I was ready, even if the path wasn't clear. The weight of transition was heavy, but it was also a necessary burden. The journey was far from over. In fact, it was only beginning.

CHAPTER 17

The Weight of Becoming

The years that followed my transition to Innisbrook were not a simple continuation of the journey I embarked upon in North East Harbor, nor were they a smooth chapter. They were a brutal, grinding recalibration of my identity. The experience was akin to entering a different realm, where the fundamental essence of my identity, the inherent structure of my existence, underwent unanticipated transformations, ones I did not predict.

I had come to this sprawling resort, with its gleaming surfaces and hidden intricacies, with the faint belief that the experience I amassed at the Asticou prepared me for what lay ahead. As months bled into years, I came to understand how terribly misguided that belief had been. I had entered a machine, a corporate beast with no interest in my history or the things I knew. It was a labyrinth that demanded more than I could give. I worked seventy hours a week, sometimes more. The days bled into each other in a haze of activity and fatigue. The physical toll was immense, yes, but what wore me down more was the constant erosion of everything I thought of leadership, service, and myself. It was exhausting, and at times, unbearable. I thought I understood the world of leadership—of guiding people, of managing operations, of leading teams to success.

During this time, I often found solace in conversations with Muffy. She was one of the few people I could truly confide in—

someone who listened without judgment, who saw through my frustrations and understood the weight I carried. I called her during long drives home or from the parking lot, venting on the impossible expectations, exhaustion, and sense of losing myself. She was always there, steady and kind, reminding me that transformation rarely feels graceful in real time.

Even as she held space for me, Muffy was facing her own battle. She was diagnosed with bladder cancer—a cruel turn that marked the beginning of a long, painful fight. It stunned me: this woman who had always been vibrant, anchored, unshakable, now standing at the edge of her own unknown. Her vulnerability deepened my respect for her. Even in her illness, she found the strength to comfort me.

Those conversations—half confession, half consolation—became a thread of sanity in a world that often made no sense. We were both unraveling in different ways, both learning how to hold grief and hope in the same breath.

At this beautiful resort, I learned in real time that leadership was more complex than I imagined. My confidence dissipated, slowly but surely, as the language of corporate hotel management, with its subtleties and layers, twisted the framework I had built for myself. I entered a world that was, in every sense, unfamiliar.

At first, I believed my straightforward, no-nonsense Russian demeanor would be an asset. I had always prided myself on my ability to be direct, to get things done, and to muscle through hard tasks, but I quickly realized that here, the bluntness that carried me through countless challenges was more of a liability than an asset. It did not belong in this world—this world of corporate precision, where everything, from how one spoke to how one held their posture, had a carefully crafted meaning. It was not strictly the words I used; it was the way I moved, the energy I projected, and the tone I struck. Everything felt strained, disconnected.

I fumbled through pre-shift meetings, stumbling to find the right words to articulate my thoughts, my expectations. I felt drawn to my native Russian—its directness, its bluntness—knowing, all the while, that it was not what the situation called for, but it was my comfort zone, my fallback strategy. On the contrary, my English, though functional, was still marked by a clumsy sharpness I could not shake. Emails became a battlefield, my tone too harsh, too cold, my sentences stiff and mechanical. My communication, once a strength, now felt like an insurmountable obstacle. I wanted to convey urgency, commitment, and clarity, but instead, it felt as though I was communicating frustration. There was a disconnect between what I intended to express and what the team received.

Worse still, I was not sure how to correct it. I was not sure who I was anymore—not as a leader, not as a woman, not as the person I thought I was. It was a crisis of self. The very foundations of who I had become were pulled from under me, and the ground beneath me, once so solid, was soft and shifting. I built an identity around the idea of being a tough, no-nonsense leader. Yet here, in this world, that identity crumbled before my eyes. I thought leadership was about managing, having answers, solving problems, being firm. But here, in this sterile, corporate world, I felt adrift, lost. Everything I thought I knew seemed irrelevant. I had no tools for this. It was in that emptiness I searched for answers.

I began to read—anything I could get my hands on. Leadership books, business philosophy, articles—anything that promised insight into the intricacies of guiding a team through the complexities of a corporate environment: *The Five Dysfunctions of a Team*, *Good to Great*, and *The 7 Habits of Highly Effective People*. I devoured them one by one, each page bringing revelations but also new questions; the more I read the more I wanted to understand. I could not help but feel that the road ahead was an endless fog, and I was stumbling through it, trying to find my way. Yet somehow, with each book,

I understood something fundamental. This was not about finding a singular, definitive answer. It was about comprehending how to question, how to break myself down and rebuild. There was no "right way." There was only my way, shaped by my experiences, my trials, and my capacity to evolve and emerge. The books I devoured were more than words on a page—they became my lifeline, my guiding principles.

The Five Dysfunctions of a Team held a mirror to my leadership, making me realize how I had isolated myself from my team with my own rigidity. It wasn't only the team I had to guide; it was myself. After every pre-shift meeting, I found myself pacing the office, testing the encumbrance of my new words, trying to speak with softness and zeal where I had once spoken with intensity and fire. The first time I tried it, I barely recognized my own voice.

"Let's keep this plain," I said to the team, my tone steady but gentle. I saw surprise in their faces. Then, slowly, with every passing sentence, the tension in the room eased. In that moment I understood—leadership wasn't forcing people to follow—it was giving them space to believe in what I was doing. More than anything, I learned this was not a path of quick fixes. It was a path of transformation, slow and sometimes painful growth, and evolution. I was not a manager anymore; I had to become a leader—not in title, but in heart. That would take time and vulnerability.

It was during this time I was handed the most terrifying challenge of all: I was offered the role of general manager of the steakhouse. The weight of the responsibility was immense. I was expected not only to oversee the daily operations of the restaurant but also to manage the business side: finances, ordering, inventory, and HR. I had handled these tasks before, but not on this scale, not in this environment. I was now expected to be the person to create and maintain systems, offer constructive criticism, guide a team that had more experience than I did.

I was overwhelmed. I had no idea what I was doing. Even more unsettling was the realization that I had been naïve to think I was ready. All my previous experience, years spent managing others, now felt irrelevant in the face of this corporate world. The complexity of it all—the politics, the expectations, the intricate web of personalities—was overwhelming. Here, amid my doubts and insecurities, I experienced another turning point.

One afternoon, after a particularly tense pre-shift meeting, Debbie, one of the longest-serving and most respected servers, pulled me aside. Her voice, always warm, carried a gravitas impossible to ignore. She spoke quietly, but every word she said cut through the haze of my confusion.

"We all care about you," she began, her eyes steady, "because we've worked alongside you for years. We want you to succeed, but the way you're leading us right now—it's not working. Your tone and your approach, it's abrasive. It makes this place feel like a battleground, and it doesn't need to be that way."

I stood frozen, struck by her honesty. I had always prided myself on being able to take criticism, but this felt different. This wasn't my performance; this was who I was becoming. Yet, in her words, there was something else: a plea for my success, a desire to see me grow.

"You don't need to be harsh," she continued. "We want you to look good because when you do, we look good. If you keep leading like this, it'll fall apart. You're the captain of the ship. You can't panic. You can't lose control. If you do, we won't follow you."

What Debbie said shook me to my core. In an instant, I saw myself as I never had before. I thought that to lead was to be strong, to be in control. What I realized, standing there in the stillness of that conversation, was that leadership was not about control—it was about trust. Giving others the confidence to follow, not through fear, but through my vision and belief. Her words were a revelatory moment.

From that moment on, I made it my mission to change. I was not sure how exactly, or even where, to begin, but I knew I had to lead from a place of compassion, of humility.

I asked Debbie to hold me accountable, to tell me if I ever crossed a line or lost my way. It was a humbling request, one that required me to be vulnerable in ways I had not been before.

It was during one of the quieter moments I felt the full weight of my isolation. I had given a directive earlier in the night to one of the servers—something that seemed simple in my mind. When the order came back wrong, the error became more than a minor issue. It felt like a failure on my part. I wanted to blame the server, to lash out with the harshness I had always relied on, but I remembered Debbie's words, ringing in my mind, *If you keep leading like this, it'll all fall apart.*

With a heavy conscience, I approached the server, not with a sharp reprimand but with a question.

"What happened?" I asked, my voice softer than I expected. As she explained the mix-up, I realized the failure was not hers—it was mine. I had not communicated clearly. The vulnerability I felt in that moment—the willingness to listen—felt like a strange, unexpected victory.

The first true test came during the PGA Tournament in March, an event that tested my patience and leadership more than anything I had faced before. The restaurant was packed with over seven hundred guests for lunch and two hundred more for dinner. The pressure was immense. As I stood in the middle of that bustling dining room, coordinating the chaos, something within me shifted. For the first time, I did not feel the crushing magnitude of fear. I felt ready. The team was ready. We had been preparing for this moment for months, and I knew, deep in my bones, that we were ready.

As I watched the restaurant bustling with activity, the energy of success tangible in the air, I realized something momentous: I had crossed a threshold. The doubt that once ruled me had melted away.

I was not the same person who arrived at Innisbrook. I discovered how to lead with patience, with empathy, with resilience. As I stood there, amid the chaos of the tournament, I realized this was no longer simply a job. It was my mission, my guiding principle. I had been forged in the fires of self-doubt, tempered by the patience of those I led, and shaped into something more. The road ahead was still long, and I had much to learn, but I felt certain of one thing: I was exactly where I needed to be.

CHAPTER 18

The Quiet Fires of Progress

The first time I saw Andy was not in a formal setting, nor was it during one of those orchestrated moments designed to impress. No, it was in the bustle of the steakhouse, a dimly lit corner booth where the air was dense with the mingling scents of wood smoke and roasting meats. He sat across from his wife, their voices soft, a perpetual flutter beneath the unwavering cadence of the restaurant. In that moment, I was not an employer seeking a chef, nor a GM scouting talent. I was a woman in sync with the vibration of the room, aware of the undercurrents flowing between people. In that fleeting glance, I felt something—a recognition, a resonance—though I couldn't yet name it. As though I had stumbled upon someone who, like me, was intricately bound to the essence of this relentless world, yet somehow still managed to remain unfazed by its weight.

I didn't know it yet, but Andy was exactly what I needed—not only for the steakhouse but for my own evolution and growth. His calm, grounded, and powerful presence conveyed the essence of his character. There was no bravado in him, no posturing. Only a steady, measured strength that would, in time, complement and tranquilize my restless energy. It wasn't simply what he could bring to the table as a chef; it was the unspoken bond that formed between us, an intuition that, if we understood each other, we could build something extraordinary.

The subsequent tasting settled the matter. Not only about complementary skill sets, it was about alignment. Our understanding of the work went beyond technique, beyond vision. It was an agreement between us, a mutual promise: we challenged each other, elevated each other, and—by dint of perseverance—pushed ourselves to heights of excellence. From the outset, our partnership felt a bit like a marriage—one built not on smooth moments but on trust shaped in the furnace of adversity. As we navigated the frenetic pace of the holidays, of Thanksgiving, Christmas, and New Year's Eve, we became something of an inseparable force.

Andy, steady as a rock in the kitchen, commanded the line with his usual poise while I maneuvered the floor of the dining room, ensuring that the guest experience remained flawless, even in the most intense moments. But the pressure was an unrelenting presence, a reminder that nothing worth achieving is ever easily attained. There were nights when the strain of it all seemed unbearable. Orders stacked in a cascade. The clock, mercilessly ticking down the seconds. We would look at each other, exhausted, questioning whether we could keep pushing, keep delivering, but in those moments, something transformative occurred. It concerned more than survival; it concerned rising to the occasion for something greater than ourselves. For the team, united in purpose.

Andy, with his understated resolve, embodied this ethos in a way that became a lesson I learned through proximity. He didn't simply manage the kitchen—he led it with dignity and patience that inspired everyone around him. And his leadership never screamed for attention. It was subtle, like the steady flow of a river carving its path through the land. He taught me that leadership was not loud commands, it cultivated a space where people thrived, evolved, and became more than what they were when they walked in.

The true test of my leadership and my growth came not in those frenetic holiday rushes but in the opening of Market Salamander

Grille. Hayato had always been the steady hand, the visionary, the one who saw potential in even the smallest idea. Market Salamander Grille was his brainchild—a bold reinvention of what Innisbrook had come to expect from on-site dining. The concept itself was a paradigm shift for its time: a farm-to-table approach with an adjacent grab-and-go market. It was more than a restaurant opening—it was a reinvention of culinary experience at the resort, innovatively ahead of its time. As we soon found out, reinvention is a process fraught with obstacles.

We had decided—out of necessity rather than brilliance—to open on Super Bowl weekend. The restaurant was packed; the influx of guests was overwhelming. We were understaffed and underprepared, yet somehow, we pushed through. The night became a blur of orders piling up, the cacophony of clinking dishes and ringing phones, each moment merged into the next like a fever dream. Plates crashed in the kitchen, the air saturated with the scent of charred meat, burned garlic, and overworked grease. The rustle of conversation from the dining room felt miles away, as though the restaurant had divided into two separate worlds—the chaos of the kitchen and the calm of the floor.

Despite the mounting pressure and the overwhelming task ahead of us, I couldn't help but notice the gleam of sweat on Sean's brow. As the manager on duty, he moved between the chaos of the line and the floor of the dining room, making sure everyone was fed, the orders were correct, and the team was functioning like a well-oiled machine. His presence, unwavering and unflappable, had become my anchor in those early days. He was a stabilizing pillar that made the overwhelming task of opening a new restaurant feel possible. It wasn't easy—not by any means—but together, we made it work.

Sean's infectious energy and unyielding humor helped lift the burden from my shoulders when the night felt endless. "Everything is groovy," he would say out of nowhere. In moments of exhaustion, when we were barely hanging on, his quick wit broke through the tension, making us all laugh when we needed it most. He was more than a colleague—he became my constant sounding board, one person I could rely on, not only for support in the moment but for perspective on the bigger picture.

During those first two weeks, I don't think I slept more than a couple of hours each night. Each evening felt like a battlefield. The dining room teemed with hundreds of patrons, while the bar was four people deep, the noise of shouted orders filling the air. The floor stretched on endlessly, an unyielding tide of faces and voices, and in the kitchen, the heat was a relentless beast. My feet ached, my knees throbbed from the hard floors, and I felt the weight of the responsibility bearing down on me, as though my very soul was being tested.

I remember Sean and I switching between expediting food and running the line, constantly recalibrating, ensuring we met every demand. The kitchen never stopped—it served three full meals a day, each period blurring into the next. There was no pause. The time between dinner and breakfast was spent cleaning, resetting, and preparing for the next round. My eyes burned with exhaustion, and my body felt like a shell of itself, no longer responding with agility. Sean, too, looked as though he had seen better days. We kept pushing—because in the rare moments of clarity, when I found myself standing beside him, watching the team work in harmony, I knew something pivotal was happening.

Sean was my constant copilot in escapades. I leaned on him when things got tough. We shared ideas, frustrations, and dreams in those moments after the mayhem subsided. We'd swap stories, sometimes laughing so much it felt like the burdens of life were momentarily forgotten. He became the first person I'd turn to when I was overwhelmed, when I needed perspective, or when a decision felt like too much to endure. It was in these tender instances of shared understanding when I realized how deeply our friendship had grown, how much we depended on each other—as teammates and as kindred spirits who saw the world with shared understanding.

He made me laugh when everything felt too serious; he could break the tension with an "off-color" joke or a story. When we did manage to carve out a moment of quiet, we'd sit together, exchanging ideas about life, philosophy, and everything. In those moments, I found comfort, support, and a sense of shared purpose that made all the frenzy worthwhile.

Getting through the service was one thing, but it was about evolving the very foundation of what we did. Clad in chef jackets, our servers seamlessly extended the culinary team, blurring the boundaries between front and back-of-house operations. It was a symbol of our unity, our shared allegiance to the endeavor. We were trying to transcend the limitations of what people expected from a restaurant of this caliber. Through it all, Sean was beside me, offering his humor and strength, reminding me that leadership was more than tough decisions—it was being human, pushing yourself to the brink, and knowing that, together, we could weather it all.

In the ever-evolving tide of my professional life, there came a presence—unexpected, yet undeniable—who helped shape what came next. Her name was Bonnie. I first encountered her during the interview process, a conversation that, at the time, seemed like another formality. There was something in her that stood apart from the others. It wasn't the polished smile or the practiced answers; it was the understated intensity in the way she spoke, the promise in the way she carried herself. She had come to us from Perkins, not with the polished resume of a fine dining veteran but with the unvarnished dedication of someone who believed in hard work above all else. That was something I respected, something I desperately needed in a world that often felt like a battle of appearances rather than true merit.

Bonnie didn't only accept the challenge of fine dining—she embraced it. She arrived with no pretense, only eagerness to learn. Her transition wasn't instantaneous. It was a gradual, determined unfolding of something more powerful than skill. It was the essence of her professionalism—the way she absorbed every lesson, every detail, every nuance with a humility that transcended any self-consciousness. Where others might falter or retreat, Bonnie leaned in. There was something of her that made you believe if she could become one of the best servers, so could anyone who applied themselves with her level of commitment.

In time, Bonnie became not only a server but a cornerstone of our team, one of the best and most dependable. She was an inexorable force in our dining room, a quiet storm that churned with precision and grace, never faltering, never wavering. She was the heart of the team—the steady pulse that kept everything moving. It wasn't long before I realized I needed her in ways I had not anticipated. The havoc of my role, the ever-shifting tides of responsibilities, demanded organization I had never quite mastered. Bonnie was that organizer, who understood systems, processes, and the delicate balance of chaos and control.

I hadn't even known how much I needed someone like her until she stepped into the role of executive assistant and coordinator. She had an uncanny ability to bring order, to see not both the big picture and every fine thread that made it whole. She who kept me focused and grounded, even when the foundation beneath me shifted. Her directness was a gift I didn't know I had been waiting for. She was always honest, despite how uncomfortable it might have been. Though her candor sometimes stung, it was a salve in the form of truth—a truth I desperately needed but had been too proud to seek on my own.

She didn't let me hide behind the façade of leadership; she forced me to grow, to confront my weaknesses, and to see where I was failing. Her logistical skill and sharp eye for detail made her indispensable, and her spirit—her unwavering belief in people made her see potential in everyone, even when they couldn't see it themselves. Bonnie's belief in people was not some idealistic fantasy; it was rooted in something far more significant. She saw the masks people wore but also the unspoken struggles behind them. While others might have become cynical or jaded by the relentless demands of the service industry, Bonnie never lost her warmth, her wholeheartedness, her unshakeable faith in the goodness of others. It was, in many ways, her dedication to others that taught me more on leadership than any book or seminar.

Bonnie was tireless in her desire to help—not only the guests who walked through our doors, but also the people she worked with. She gave so much of herself, often at her own expense, always putting others first even when it drained her. She had no need for validation, no desire for accolades; she simply did what was right, because, in her world, that was enough. She was willing to sacrifice pieces of herself for the collective good, yet somehow, she never hardened in the process. Her spirit remained untainted, even when the world tried to erode it.

Bonnie taught me kindness in a profound way, without ever speaking a word about it. She was a paradox, a balance of fire and gentleness, a reminder that true strength wasn't always loud or obvious—it was the reposeful, constant commitment to doing what was right, regardless of the cost. She was the type of person who, no matter the circumstance, always found the good in others and extended her hand, even when it seemed unreciprocated. She never became bitter, never closed herself off. Instead, she grew. Her kindness became an unruffled rebellion against the hardness the world often demanded. Even when we disagreed, when our paths seemed at odds, Bonnie's presence was a constant. She stayed, like a calm center in a storm, reminding me that despite how difficult or frustrating things became, there was always room for growth, for understanding. She wasn't afraid to challenge me, to push me past my comfort zones, to see things through a different lens.

It was through these differences that we forged a bond transcending professional ties. Bonnie became one of my closest friends, a woman whose strength and determination I admired, whose belief in me kept me grounded. In the end, true leadership does not make decisions from a place of power. It makes them from a place of shared experience, vulnerability, and respect. It recognizes the strengths in others, even when they cannot see them themselves. It creates spaces where people are free to grow, even when it seems uncomfortable.

> ***Leadership creates space for freedom***
> ***to grow, even through discomfort.***

I learned from Andy, Sean, Hayato, and Bonnie. They are not only leaders but individuals who, through their actions, showed me that leadership is a reflection of who we are, how we treat others, and how we choose to show up day after day. When the dust settles, those inconspicuous fires of progress are the ones that burn the brightest.

CHAPTER 19

Leading with Humanity, an Ongoing Journey

The kitchen was upstairs, always alive, always pulsing with its own whirr. The air, thick with food and heat, vibrated with an energy both relentless and full of purpose. In clear contrast, the managers' offices were down in the basement—cold, sterile, and lit by harsh, flickering fluorescent lights. The space was small, wedged into the farthest corner of a sea of cubicles. The door opened into a larger room where the other managers worked, though none were there now. I sat at my desk, surrounded by papers, schedules, and numbers.

Far removed from the immediate demands of the kitchen, this place allowed for some distance, both from the people I led and the pressures they brought. Yet, the stillness in this office, thick and heavy, didn't offer the relief I hoped for. Instead, it pressed against me—suffocating in its quiet. The weight of it wasn't physical but existential, a rare and unwelcome pause, one that forced me to confront the full expanse of the leadership I inherited and the leadership I attempted to shape.

I leaned back in my chair and ran my hand across my face. It felt like an age ago I had taken on this role, this mantle of responsibility. As I looked around, I realized I hadn't stopped to consider the meaning of this journey for a long time. The office itself, the sterile silence, felt like a space carved out for reflection, but even here, I struggled to find clarity.

Leadership, I knew, was never simple. It wasn't a matter of making decisions or directing others. It wasn't even about the accomplishments, the numbers, or the visible success. Leadership was. It was, in its truest sense, a living, breathing organism—a powerful equilibrium of vulnerability, pride and humility, success and failure. At times, a burden too heavy to carry, but other moments revealed it as a privilege—an opportunity to shape not only the course of others' work but their lives.

As I sat there, the world above felt distant, like a memory. The noise that once defined my leadership approach seemed far removed from the quiet, reflective space I now found myself in. How many years had I spent thinking leadership was about visibility, control, constant forward momentum? How much had I overlooked in my pursuit of success, the whirlwind of meetings, objectives, and deadlines?

I thought of a manager who left my office that afternoon, his face stern, his demeanor impatient, his eyes always moving from one task to the next. He was efficient, quick—undeniably effective. As he walked out, I couldn't shake the impression that something essential was missing. There had been no connection, no acknowledgment of the people he led, no effort to understand what drove them, what inspired them. His leadership was mechanical—an automated process—and I wondered: how often had I been guilty of the same?

It wasn't the first time I'd encountered such a style of leadership, but it was a moment when I realized something about myself. There had been times in my career when I, too, had been more concerned with the task at hand than with the people who carried it out. I assumed if I could get the work done, if I pushed harder and managed more efficiently, the results would follow. Leadership, I had come to understand, wasn't about execution. It was about people, their needs, and the spaces we created for them to grow.

My thoughts drifted to a conversation I once had with a mentor—a moment that changed my view on leadership entirely. She had told me, matter-of-factly, that the very people who worked the hardest for you—the ones who sacrificed, who excelled—were the ones we kept in place, tethered to roles where we needed them. We didn't reward them by promoting them or giving them the opportunities they sought. Instead, we kept them there, as if exceptional performance were a reason to punish them, to ensure we could rely on them.

It struck me then: Why would we not reward those who showed exceptional ability? Why not give them the opportunity to grow, to ascend to higher positions? The realization hit hard. She was right. I had kept people in roles where they performed well because I needed them. But in doing so, I wasn't fostering their development; I was stifling it. I wasn't rewarding their loyalty and excellence; I was taking advantage of it. I had been leading out of necessity rather than generosity.

That conversation altered my perspective. It forced me to question the true nature of leadership. Leadership does not hoard talent, use people as tools for our goals. It sees the potential in others and nurtures it, even when that means letting go of the very people we rely on. It is fair, but with a nuanced, individualized perspective. Leadership demands we treat people according to their individual needs, aspirations, and contributions, not with a blanket approach that benefits us.

So I reshaped my stance. I realized I had to treat people fairly, not equally. If someone performed at a higher level, they deserved more—not in terms of reward, but in opportunity, in development, in attention. They deserved the space to grow, to move beyond their current roles, even if it meant losing them. I would no longer punish them by keeping them in places they had outgrown. Instead, I would reward them by pushing them to new heights, even at the risk of losing them.

I thought back to times I had failed as a leader—when I had been driven by outcomes, by numbers, by the fear of losing control. Those were the moments when I had treated people as tools, when I had neglected their growth because I needed them where they were. Leadership isn't simply about getting the work done. It creates the conditions in which others can thrive—not just professionally, but as people. It encourages their development, even when it makes things uncomfortable, even when it feels like a sacrifice on our part.

> ***Leadership creates conditions for others to thrive.***

Through all of this, I've come to understand that leadership is a continuous journey. It's not about perfection or being right all the time; it's about showing up with humility, with vulnerability, and with an allegiance to the people you lead. Embrace the complexities, the contradictions, and the struggles that come with guiding others, not from a place of authority but from a place of shared experience. Leadership, in the end, does not command others to follow. It walks beside them, understanding their individual needs, and helps them achieve what they thought was out of reach. It creates an environment where people feel valued—not only for what they do, but for who they are.

So, as I sat there, in the stillness of my office in the basement, I realized I was still learning. There were days when I got it right and days when I failed. When all was said and done, it wasn't the destination that mattered, it was the journey. At its core, leadership is a ceaseless transformation that requires not only guiding others but also guiding oneself through the complexities of human connection, resilience, and growth. It's not about being the smartest, the most accomplished, or the most successful. It's about showing up, engaging fully—every single day—and leading with empathy, with patience, and with a genuine desire to help others be the best versions of themselves. I continue this journey, unsure of where it will lead but committed to the path: lead with humanity, grow alongside the people I lead, and always remember that the crux of leadership lies in the connections we make, the trust we build, and the lives we touch.

CHAPTER 20

The Beginning of Something Grand

When Andy and I first arrived at Salamander Middleburg Virginia in early August, the sun still hung heavily in the sky, casting a warm glow over the sprawling estate. We were part of a task force team assembled to open the resort—an ambitious endeavor that felt both exhilarating and daunting. Though our home base remained Florida and this was only a temporary assignment, the air was thick with the heavy promise of late summer, but there was a whisper of fall in the breeze, enough to remind you that change was coming.

The rolling Virginia hills stretched out in every direction, the vineyards a patchwork of green and bronze, the Blue Ridge Mountains looming majestically in the distance. It felt like we were stepping into a dream—a place both timeless and rooted in the here and now. This was a very different feel from the one I had grown accustomed to in Palm Harbor, Florida.

The resort itself, nestled quietly among the trees, looked less like a hotel and more like a grand country estate. The structure was imposing yet graceful, with two wings flanking a central courtyard that seemed castle-like in its proportions. As we walked through the entrance, the world outside disappeared. We were not walking into a cold, impersonal lobby but rather into someone's home—a home of unimaginable luxury, to be sure, but still a home.

The moment you stepped into the living room, you felt it—a warmth, a welcoming that reached out and enveloped you. The space was enormous but intimately designed, with three grand fireplaces casting flickering light across plush, inviting seating. Expensive carpets were carefully rolled out, and artwork, still being hung on the walls, added a touch of elegance that only spoke to the refinement of the place. Despite the construction in every corner, the space didn't feel unfinished. It felt like a house under the finishing touches—small adjustments, tiny moments of artistry, all pointing toward the perfection soon to come.

The massive windows, stretching from floor to ceiling, framed the grand lawn like a living painting. The view was too perfect—expansive and green, dotted with flower beds and sweeping pathways that led toward the horizon. Inside, the air smelled faintly of fresh paint and new wood—both the scent of luxury and the scent of something still becoming. It felt like the calm before a storm, the sort of place where you could imagine royalty walking through the halls, yet it remained grounded, as though it were the home of one of your wealthiest friends, someone who knew how to make you feel right at ease despite the grandeur of their surroundings.

We made our way past the living room, now mostly finished, toward the heart of the operation—the kitchen. It was there we found Hayato and Wayne, two pillars of our opening team. As we stepped into the back of the house, the familiar buzz of pre-opening chaos greeted us—the sound of clattering boxes and the shuffle of hurried feet. The kitchen was a labyrinth of unopened crates, piled high with everything from fine china to silverware, glassware, and kitchen equipment. It felt like a warehouse, not a space meant for culinary brilliance. There was no smell of fresh-baked bread or sizzling meats, only the sharp, sterile scent of boxes and packaging tape.

The dining room, too, was a mess of scattered furniture and unfinished details; nothing was in its place. Not a trace of the grand dining tables, and the servers' stations were bare. In the middle of this, Wayne was hunched over a stack of papers at the makeshift desk, his brow furrowed as he went through the initial opening paperwork. He was at ease, poised as always, but his focus was unshakable. As soon as he saw us, he put the papers down and walked over, his presence calm but urgent.

He had not changed—the same Wayne, that constant source of steady wisdom, but now, he was immersed in the reality of the moment, managing the mountain of logistics that needed conquering in the coming days.

"We're seventeen days out," he said quietly, shaking his head as if the reality of it was sinking in for him too. "We're going to need more hands."

The sobering truth hit hard. The hotel was not yet ready, and we still did not have our licenses. We were so close, yet there was so much left to do. There were no chefs plating intricate dishes or waitstaff rehearsing their steps—just us, unboxing and unpacking, laying a strong foundation for what soon became a luxury experience. It was a race against time, and it was not clear if we would make it to the finish line without a few stumbles along the way.

Wayne, calm as ever, took a deep breath, and without missing a beat, jumped behind the dishwasher to begin washing the last of the pre-opening china. It was a move that only someone with his level of humility and hands-on experience could make. There was no task too small or beneath him in this moment. Meanwhile, Andy and I turned to the piles of boxes, starting the exhausting and endless process of organizing everything that would make the opening possible. The clock was ticking, but all we could do was keep moving forward.

"Let's get started," I said to Andy, pulling up my sleeves. "We've got a lot of work to do." We worked in silence for a while, each of us lost in our own thoughts. The air around us buzzed with the urgency that only the last stretch of a pre-opening period can bring.

Amid it all, there was an underlying excitement too—a thrill at what would unfold. Despite the overwhelming nature of the task, the thought of what Salamander Middleburg would become kept us going, even if the path ahead was murky. With every box we opened, every dish we washed, I felt the dream beginning to take shape, even if it were only in disjointed parts for now. As I looked around at the people working alongside me—Wayne, Andy, Hayato—I knew that, together, we would make it happen. No matter the number of days or late nights, we would succeed.

After a sixteen-hour workday, Andy and I were utterly drained—our bodies sore, minds still reeling from the endless unboxing and last-minute adjustments. The sense of urgency had not subsided, but a quiet exhaustion had set in, pulling at us in ways only opening-day rush can. The place, still unfinished, started to reveal its grandeur, like a diamond being carefully cut and polished.

Around midnight, when the rest of the team had called it a night, we decided to venture out and take a much-needed break. The spa was the one place in the resort that had taken on its full form, and we were eager to see it in its near-final state. As we entered the spa, the change in atmosphere was immediate. Gone was the frantic energy of construction and chaos. Instead, the air was thick with peace, nearly tangible.

The entrance was grand, yet inviting, like stepping into a serene sanctuary. A cascading water feature greeted us with its gentle, soothing sound, setting the tone for the rest of the space. Above the arrival desk hung an exquisite piece of art, each stroke deliberate, thoughtfully placed as if it had always belonged. The chandelier in the vestibule was breathtaking—delicate, yet commanding, casting intricate shadows across the space. It was a dance between opulence and calm, a place that exuded beauty without overwhelming the senses.

The skylight above bathed the space in cool moonlight, and I paused in the relentless rush of the day. Time slowed down here, only for a few minutes.

We were so used to the noise, the movement, and the pressure of deadlines that this stillness felt like a foreign luxury. It was quiet, too quiet, and for a moment, I felt like I had stepped into another world altogether.

I turned my attention to the relaxation room, and it was nothing short of otherworldly. Italian tile covered the walls and ceilings, its colors—deep, warm tones of terracotta and gold—giving the entire room its own glow. The scent of lavender and eucalyptus lingered in the air, mixed with the unmistakable clean, fresh smell of new stone. The loungers, made of mini tiles in light blue hues, gleamed under the ambient lighting. They were heated—subtle warmth radiating from them, an invitation to sink into complete relaxation.

Andy, alternatively, was already beyond the point of exhaustion. His back, stiff from hours of work, was in agony. He sank down onto one of the beautiful loungers, and the warmth immediately worked its magic. A contented sigh escaped him, the kind that only comes when you've been working for hours on end and finally allow yourself to sink into true comfort. He closed his eyes, his shoulders dropped, and within minutes, the tension melted away. He was practically drifting into a nap, his face softening in the peacefulness of the space.

I smiled to myself, happy to see him so relaxed. Yet I was drawn to discover more. Quietly, I moved through the spa, pausing at each corner to take it in, to remember.

The treatment rooms were tucked away behind frosted glass doors, each one more luxurious than the last. I stumbled upon a couples room, and it bewildered me. It had its own private bath, a jacuzzi that invited you to sink into its bubbles, and a small, intimate patio outside under the open sky. The moonlight reflected off the water, casting a glow on the stone walls and the verdant greenery beyond. The spa extended into the open air, where a stunning infinity pool awaited. Its edge disappeared into the rolling Virginia countryside, a seamless transition between water and earth. The view from here was something out of a painting, with the moon hanging low over the horizon, casting silver light across the landscape, tendrils of steam drifting lazily off the warm pool.

The cabanas around the pool were quiet, waiting for guests to enjoy this beauty. The travertine pavers around the pool shimmered, untouched, their warm tones soft in the night. There was something indescribable about the place at that hour. It was unmarked, perfect, waiting, as though it were on the cusp of something incredible. The world outside seemed miles away, and the noise of the construction seemed to have never existed in this tranquil oasis.

I sat for a moment on the edge of the pool, letting the peace of the place wash over me, imagining how it would feel once it was open—full of life, full of guests who came here to escape, to breathe, to be pampered. An electric charge, hinting at the magic this place would soon bring to life, filled the air with anticipation. For now, it was only me, the stars, the calm, and the stillness of something extraordinary.

When I finally returned to Andy, he was fast asleep, his face relaxed in a way I hadn't seen in days. I chuckled softly, aware he'd be eager to resume the pace in the morning, but for now, we savored a rare moment before reemerging into the world. As I turned to leave, I gave the spa one last look. It was almost ready—almost perfect—and I felt a deep sense of pride. All the hours, the work, the stress—it would all be worth it. The Salamander would be something unforgettable. Tonight, it was a beautiful, tranquil dream.

The days leading up to the opening were a blur of exhaustion and elation, where each passing hour stretched beyond reason, as if time itself had taken a life of its own. In those final days, when the resort was a skeleton of its intended grandeur—unfinished walls, scattered boxes, the rumble of preparation in every corner—I found myself pushed to the limits of both body and mind. Yet, I was not alone.

There were others whose strength, determination, and grace carried the magnitude of this monumental opening in ways that shaped my understanding of both the task at hand and the people I had come to rely on. Giana, with her poised, unflinching resolve, was a constant presence in those late-night hours. Together, alongside Tatum, we formed a strange fellowship—misfits, each of us driven by ambition that bordered on obsession, bound by a shared understanding that we were creating something larger than ourselves. During those moments, when the walls remained empty and the resort's vision lingered solely in our thoughts, our collaborative efforts went beyond establishing a hotel. There were tender moments of shared labor, subtle understanding between those who worked side by side, driven by a singular goal.

I remember Giana and me in the cooking studio at two in the morning, stocking shelves with pots, pans, and retail items. The space was in disarray, its potential not realized, but we worked with a focus that made everything else fade. We arranged and reorganized, making it look like the set of a culinary television show, knowing that in less than ten hours, the resort would open its doors to guests. We were delirious from days of unbroken work, yet in those moments, there was no place I would have rather been. Giana, ever the steady hand, ensured we stayed on task, making sure the shelves looked arranged by professionals, while I flitted between various duties, distracted by the enormity of the tasks. I saw in her the embodiment of leadership—quiet, strong, and unwavering. She constantly guided us with a focus I admired.

Tatum, with her own vibrant energy, balanced Giana's calm with a humor and wit both disarming and inspiring. Ambitious and driven, she commanded the banquet department with effortless grace, orchestrating every detail with precision. She was the type of leader who commanded attention without saying a word—her presence alone was enough to ensure everything was done to perfection. Her ability to lead and her infectious personality set her apart. Tatum had a way of making the most difficult moments manageable, often with a sarcastic remark or a knowing glance. She reminded us we could laugh even in the worst situations. Her leadership was something I looked to as an example, something I knew I could draw from as the days wore on.

Then there was Mimi, who brought calm yet powerful authority to everything she touched. With her background in Washington's finest restaurants, she understood luxury both rare and invaluable. As the in-room dining manager, Mimi did not simply oversee a team, she shaped it. She saw potential where others saw only mistakes and cultivated that potential into something extraordinary. She embodied a perfect blend of grace and grit, managing job pressures with poise and demonstrating deep care for the people she worked with. I learned more from her than I can express—about leadership, about service, and about the quiet power of mentorship.

Becky came into her role as restaurant director with a calm that defied the frenetic energy of the pre-opening. A true Southern belle, her approach to hospitality was nothing short of refined. She embodied grace, poise, and unwavering commitment—qualities that made her seem worlds apart from the rest of us, who ran on fumes, looking every bit the part of the frantic, sleep-deprived souls we were. While we all stumbled through the frenzy, Becky was always perfectly put together, as though she had somehow found a way to escape the madness. She carried a serenity that made the pressure manageable. Her composure struck me but also her uncanny ability to anticipate the needs of others, to take care of things before they were asked of her. I will never forget the moment she pulled an electric tea kettle from her "Mary Poppins" bag, saving me from my endless complaints about not having one. It was a small gesture, but it encapsulated who Becky was—thoughtful, resourceful, and always ready to step in and make things better, regardless of how impossible it seemed.

Together, these individuals formed the foundation of a team that was greater than the sum of its parts. Each of us contributed unique perspectives and individually shaped the experience. They were not my anchors—they were the winds and the sails that pushed me forward, each influencing me in their own way. Wayne, steady and calm, an expert in operations, guided us through many complexities with quiet authority. Hayato, relentless in his diligence, organized with a grace that made it look effortless. Andy, my loyal companion, was always there when I needed him, providing a steady, grounding presence when the pressure became too much.

In the end, the collective effort of everyone—their individual strengths, their dedication, their craftsmanship—created something extraordinary. The resort we constructed was more than a physical structure; it was a manifestation of our collective vision, the result of our unwavering dedication, and the close relationships we forged during the critical moments.

As we stood there, hours before opening the doors to the world, I knew what we had created was something that would outlast us all—a legacy not only of luxury but of those who sparked its existence.

CHAPTER 21

Unveiling the Dream

The morning of August 29 broke like a quiet promise, the sun's soft light spilling over the Blue Ridge Mountains as though nature was eager to witness the birth of something earth-shattering. The air felt thick with anticipation, like the stillness that precedes monumental moments—suspended, almost sacred. The resort stood as though holding its breath, the fading moments before we finally admitted the world inside.

I stood in the grand lobby, my fingers grazing the smooth marble columns, allowing myself a fleeting moment of reflection. The scent of lavender from the garden mixed with freshly polished wood. It was the smell of something that had been nurtured, carefully crafted, with every detail given its due. Today was not only the opening of a hotel, it was the culmination of countless hours of hopes and dreams woven into a physical space. Salamander was no longer an idea; it had become something living, with its own heartbeat.

Each inch of the resort, from its soaring ceilings to the intricate details in the furniture, was constructed with intention, with devotion, with an unwavering pursuit of perfection. The layers upon layers of design—subtle, bold, and elegant—melded in seamless harmony. From the warm leather seats to the luscious mahogany adorning the walls, everything was in its rightful place, yet it all felt timeless, as though this place had always existed. The clock was ticking—each passing minute pulling us closer to the grand moment of the ribbon-cutting ceremony. The final touches were added, silver polished to a mirror-like sheen, glasses stacked in perfect alignment, and the gentle jingle of utensils signaled the imminent arrival of guests. The space was coming alive in an almost-spiritual way. It was no longer the mere product of our work—it was the manifestation of collective vision. Today, the dream stepped beyond its shadowed beginnings into vivid life.

Even as the physical space came to life, it was the intangible spirit of Salamander that was perhaps most extraordinary. There was a shared excitement humming in the air, a palpable sense of unity among the team. We were no longer individuals working toward a goal; we had become something more. Fatigue was inescapable—after all, this was the final stretch of an opening that tested our limits—but in the mayhem and frantic energy, there was also a calm understanding that we were all part of something larger than ourselves. This was our creation.

In the final countdown, we brought into existence something with far greater significance than its individual components. The flash mob, choreographed for the owner's arrival, became a metaphor for the energy and camaraderie among us. Over two hundred staff members, some with two left feet, others with surprising rhythm, lined the circular drive to perform an impromptu dance. The aim was not to surprise her—it was to show what we had become. This moment was a testament to our shared mission, a spontaneous expression of joy, a celebration of the collective spirit that had driven us through the sleepless nights and long days. As the music pulsed and we moved in perfect unison, something magical happened. For those few minutes, the weight, the pressure, and the nerves—all of it melted away. There was only the music, the movement, and the shared joy of being part of this moment. In that instance, everything that led us to that point came together in harmony.

The ribbon-cutting ceremony was less a formal event than a collective exhalation. The champagne corks popped in celebration, but it wasn't only the bubbly that marked the occasion. It was the sense we had done something extraordinary. As the ribbon fell and the doors opened wide, the resort breathed its first as a living entity. We—the team who poured our souls into it—stood there, hearts beating in time with the pulse of the space.

The resort was not a collection of buildings; it was home. It had become the embodiment of dedication, of sacrifice, of sleepless nights. There was an energy that transcended the physical; it was a place that spoke to something deeper and enduring. Guests slowly trickled in, each one marveling at the space as though stepping into a dream. The air hummed with newness and excitement, and it was in those first moments when I realized this hotel had been created not with bricks and mortar but with stories, moments, and collective effort.

I walked through the spaces—the Herriman's Grill, the wine bar, the grand ballroom—marveling at how each room held its own unique personality, yet everything perfectly coordinated as if the hotel itself was telling a story. The Herriman's Grill, with its barn-inspired octagonal design, evoked warmth and history, paying homage to the Piedmont region's agricultural heritage. Every corner of the restaurant had been thoughtfully curated, from the elegant table linens to the small purse stools designed for each guest—a minor touch, but one that spoke volumes of the care and thought we poured into every detail.

It was the restaurant where beauty and thoughtfulness were woven into the fabric of the resort. Everywhere I looked, there were moments of quiet awe—fresh flowers adorning every corner, each room reflecting a different season, like nature itself had been invited inside. A local artist's stunning equestrian artwork—oil paintings that breathed life into the walls—lined the corridors. These works of art spoke to the region's history and the resort's spirit—strong, yet graceful; timeless, yet vibrant.

As I walked through the guest rooms, each felt like a retreat from the world. It was not about the luxury or the comfort; it was about the design. Each floor represented a different season, a reflection of the cycles of nature—spring, summer, fall, and winter. The rooms on each floor embodied that season's essence, through color and texture, through the atmosphere they created. The artwork adorning the walls was not equestrian this time; instead, it was photography—a homage to our owner's vision and spirit. Every room was an intimate space, offering guests a sense of peace—a space to reflect, retreat, and escape the outside world. The floors of the hotel, with carefully curated designs, mirrored my own journey—each season representing a step along the path of growth, of change, of becoming. The wool carpets beneath my feet, the soft leather chairs, the mahogany accents—all felt like a reflection of the journey we had undertaken together. It was a journey of building something more than a place; we had built a destination, an experience, a living testament to what could be achieved when a group of people worked together toward a shared goal.

The common spaces—the library adjacent to the living room, the grand lawn surrounded by the beautiful Virginia woods—felt like extensions of the rooms themselves. The library was full of books, each shelf a tender invitation to step into a new world. The light filtered through the large windows that faced the lawn, where guests gathered around the fire pits, sipped cocktails, or indulged in s'mores kits created by our pastry team. These small touches—simple yet significant—added depth to the experience. They were a reminder that luxury did not always have to be grand. Sometimes, it was in the unanticipated moments of joy—the laughter shared by guests around the fire, the smell of freshly baked goods wafting through the air—that Salamander authentically revealed its soul.

***

As the days wore on, and the resort became a destination in its own right, the beauty of the place took root. The culinary team, led by Chef Chris, a Michelin-starred talent, created dishes that were not mere meals but experiences. Jason, the pastry chef, consistently innovated his craft, resulting in each dessert being more inventive than the previous one. The culinary garden, the on-site bee farm (apiary), and the equestrian stables—all became integral parts of the Salamander experience.

The resort was alive, its beauty reflected not only in the design and the food, but in the people who inhabited it. Standing on the grand lawn that first evening as the sun set, I felt reposeful satisfaction. The warmth of the late summer air, the scent of the earth beneath my feet, and the sound of laughter and conversation filling the air—it all reminded me that Salamander was more than a luxury resort. It was shaped by our hands and hearts as we worked so hard to create it. This was not a hotel; it was a dream realized. As I stood there amid laughter, fire pits, s'mores, elegance, and joy, I was certain we had accomplished something extraordinary. We created a place where stories would unfold, memories would be made, and the dream that began with a single vision was now a living, breathing reality.

CHAPTER 22

Between Waves and Walls: A New Horizon

As the sun dipped beneath the horizon, spilling streaks of crimson and amber across the sky, I sat on the soft, cool sand of Siesta Key beach, the waves whispering secrets as they lapped at the shore. Muffy, beside me, the steady anchor of calm in my life, held my hand loosely, her touch a quiet assurance that no words captured. We had done this countless times before, sitting together in the late afternoon, watching the world around us transform as the day gave way to dusk. Today felt different. The transition felt deeper, more radical, as if the sea itself had been reflecting my inner world—its restlessness, its calm, its endless ebb, and its flow.

In the still moments—the moments between milestones—I felt the stirrings of something I could not ignore. Life beyond the hotel's walls had been growing louder, until it demanded my attention. I was tired—tired of the constant rush, tired of the constant need to prove myself, tired of pushing myself further, faster, and higher. More than that, I realized that in the quest to build monumental things, I had neglected the very thing that grounded me in a deeper, more lasting sense of fulfillment: the possibility of a family.

I looked out over the water, its surface shimmering like liquid glass, reflecting the last remnants of sunlight. Muffy, sensing the change within me, had become my steady presence, my grounding force.

She witnessed the unfolding of my career—the successes and the struggles—yet she never wavered in her belief in me. Her unruffled strength was something I had come to rely on, and in this moment, I knew I was ready to confront the truth brewing within me for months.

"Do you ever wonder, Muffy," I asked, my voice faint, lost to the sound of the waves, "if it's all enough? All this building, all this striving? I've done so much, and yet, I feel like something is missing. What is it?"

Muffy turned to me, her weathered face softening in the light of the setting sun. Her eyes, always so steady and full of understanding, met mine, and for a moment, she didn't speak, as if allowing the weight of the question to settle between us.

"It's not what you've built or conquered, poopsy," she said, using the sweet nickname she always called me, her voice cloaked in the affection I had come to cherish. "It is what you've yet to create. What is waiting to bloom in the space you've carved out for yourself? The heart, the soul, the part of you that has always been hidden beneath the walls you built around it."

I sat in silence for a long while, her words settling deep within me.

What had I been building all these years? Was it a career? Or was it an escape? I had invested so much of myself into my work, into the pursuit of excellence, that I had forgotten what it felt like to long for something apart from the office, outside of the never-ending deadlines. What did it mean to be a mother, a partner, a woman not defined by her job?

As the questions swirled within me, I felt the pull of something new. A new horizon beckoned, not only as a professional but as a woman prepared to embark on a distinct legacy. One not built from polished marble and pristine glass but shaped by love, by family, by the very essence of life itself.

"I've always defined myself by what I've done, Muffy," I said, my voice barely above a whisper. "But I do not know who I am without it. I do not know who I am when I'm not in a boardroom, or on a construction site, or managing a team."

Muffy smiled gently, squeezing my hand. "Then it's time to learn. Time to redefine yourself, not by the walls you built, but by the life you want to create."

It felt as though a load was lifted from my core.

There was no clear path ahead, no manual to follow for this next stage of life, but I felt an overwhelming sense of peace wash over me. The waves continued to the shore, each one retreating only to return, each one a reminder that the journey was not linear, that growth came in cycles, and that the horizon would always remain, beckoning me to step forward.

I sat beside Muffy, the sun's rays casting long shadows across the sand. I realized I was at a crossroads, not only in my career but in my identity. It wasn't the legacy of Salamander Resort that called to me now. It was the legacy of who I was becoming outside of work, outside of expectations, outside of pressures. I spent many years building others' dreams. Now, for the first time, I was ready to build my own.

In that moment, the truth of Muffy's words settled in: It wasn't about what I had built, but what I had yet to create. The family I wanted to raise. The child I longed to welcome into my life. The reverence and joy that would fill my home during quiet, everyday moments. Balance. Finding the harmony between the waves of ambition that had carried me this far and the walls that now created a sanctuary for the life I wanted to nurture. The horizon was not far. In fact, it was within my reach.

There are moments in life when time seems to stand still, when the weight of a decision or a shift in the course of one's journey becomes so life-altering you cannot escape its implications, no matter how hard you try. My life, as I now understood it, had been a series of such moments—milestones passed in quick succession, each a battle, each a victory, but also, each an inadvertent step farther away from the very things I once thought I wanted. It had been two years since I sat on that beach with Muffy and first whispered the truth aloud—I wanted to be a mother.

It was not until I became a mother that I fully understood the complexities of duality, of being torn between two forces that, though intertwined, never fully coexisted in harmony. I spent many years building and conquering—pushing myself further into my career with each project, each hotel, and each challenge. But motherhood—nothing prepared me for the weight of it, nor the fierce, all-encompassing love that surged through me when I first held my son in my arms.

Pregnancy, in all its beauty and complexity, arrived quickly, as if life had decided I had been pushing myself long enough. I was pregnant before I had a chance to consider the gravity of what that meant. There was no slowing down. Not for my career, not for my ambition. I worked through every stage of my pregnancy, refusing to take any break or heed the cautions of my body, pushing myself to meet deadlines and lead my teams with the same intensity that always defined me. The discomforts were numerous—catching the swine flu early in my pregnancy left me weakened, my body battling against both the illness and the strain of growing a child within me. Then, there was the rare skin condition that had me writhing in agony from the incessant itching, so intense that I longed for the sweet release of fire to scorch away the torment. Still, I pressed forward, for there was no room for stillness in my world—not when there were so many things to build and so many people relying on me.

July 10, 2012, the day I gave birth, felt like the culmination of this never-ending drive. I continued working until the final moments, on the Sunday preceding my Tuesday delivery. I seamlessly transitioned from meetings, deadlines, and calls to the frenzy of labor, treating it like any other project I had to oversee. The birth itself, though beautiful, felt like the beginning of another cycle in my relentless pursuit of excellence—an unwelcome shift I was not yet ready to face. I had been raised to believe in strength, in resilience. My Russian roots held a deeply ingrained taboo against weakness, vulnerability, and admitting when something was too much.

So, despite the overwhelming exhaustion, despite the tender fragility of early motherhood, I ignored the early signs of postpartum, convinced that if I pushed harder, if I muscled through, I would be fine. But I wasn't fine.

Eight weeks. Eight weeks was all I allowed myself for maternity leave—barely enough to bond with my newborn son. I could not afford to slow down—I couldn't afford to lose the momentum I had worked so hard to build. I returned to work way too soon, a frantic attempt to prove that I could juggle both worlds—motherhood and career—without falling apart. It was an illusion, of course. I was falling apart in ways I did not even fully understand at the time. My mother came to help, as mothers do, offering what support she could, but her presence, while invaluable, created tensions in my relationship.

The balance that I had so desperately sought in my life was slipping through my fingers, like sand on the beach. Despite my efforts to maintain balance, a part of me, rooted in my primal nature, clung to the belief I could still achieve it all. That was the lie I told myself. I bought my first house, a symbol of a life I had built, and yet, every step of that journey felt like a negotiation with myself. I was never fully present for my family; my mind was always elsewhere—on the next meeting, the next deadline, the next hotel opening. I was constantly pulling away from the ones I loved, telling myself it was for their future, for their security, but deep down, I knew it was not. It was for something else—some unspoken, never-satisfied ambition.

Then there was breastfeeding. The pumping sessions at work, the endless coordination of trying to nourish my son while managing my career—it was a monumental task—but it was one I took on without question because I had always been someone who did. I didn't have the luxury of asking for help or expecting accommodations. The world, and the corporate structures I navigated, did not cater to women like me—the women who sought to be everything to everyone. Yet, I continued to push, even as I faltered in my own life.

Through all the challenges—the sleepless nights, the moments of self-doubt, the remorse clawed at me when I wasn't there for my son or my partner. I realized something weighty: the ardor I felt for my child eclipsed every accomplishment, every project, every success I had ever known. As I watched him grow, as I saw him learn and develop into his own person, I understood that nothing in my life compared to the joy of being his mother.

Yet, the struggle to balance that love with my ambition—the tension between the two—was something I could not easily resolve. I saw how I had failed, how my work ethic, my refusal to step back, had cost me so much. I was not present for my partner, for my family, and I wasn't present for myself. There was a growing realization—one that echoed through the quiet moments and late nights—that, despite my success and everything I built, I was losing something infinitely more valuable. That awareness took time to sink in because my career and self-imposed expectations continued to rule my life. I was not the person I thought I was. I was not the person my family needed me to be.

CHAPTER 23

The Vicious Cycle

The whirlwind of my life continued to spin relentlessly, its dizzying pace masking the cracks that had begun to widen in both my professional and personal worlds. On the surface, I was managing. On paper, everything looked perfectly aligned. I was an image of success, a leader in my industry, carving out a legacy that seemed as substantial as the glass and steel structures I built. Yet beneath the polished exterior, deep dissonance grew. The internal turmoil I could not escape masticated at me in every calm moment, and I spent countless sleepless nights replaying the same thoughts, the same worries, the same relentless drive to push through.

At work, I immersed myself in ever-growing demands. The stakes were high, the pressure suffocating. It wasn't the job—it was the unrelenting need to prove I could keep up, handle it all, even when everything in my life felt like it was spiraling out of control. As I juggled high-profile events and VIP guests, a part of me still longed to connect with something more—something real. Those moments felt fleeting, fragile wisps of light in an otherwise dark tunnel.

I buried myself in work, in deadlines, in managing the constant cadence of the hotel's operations, while knowing that each passing day took me one step closer to losing Muffy. I hadn't gone to see her that year. Each passing month, I promised myself I would visit, but something always stood in the way—work commitments, my own exhaustion, the unease that festered within me, knowing I wasn't ready to confront the unavoidable. The truth was I didn't want to see her slipping away. I couldn't bear the idea of seeing her, once so full of life, reduced to a shadow of herself, battling cancer and weakened by the relentless toll of chemotherapy.

As her memory faded, I still tried to reach her. I tried to hold on to the Muffy I had known as she slipped further into the fog of illness. I would call sometimes, and the voice on the other end of the line—so familiar, yet so altered—would struggle to form coherent thoughts. The cancer ravaged her body, and the medication to manage the pain left her confused and disoriented. Sometimes, she wouldn't recognize my voice. She would laugh softly, childlike, and I heard the disconnect in her tone. It was heartbreaking, shattering, to witness the loss of someone who had been my anchor, my confidante, my constant source of wisdom.

Yet, in the middle of all of it, there was Jeff. Jeff was the man who loved Muffy, truly and deeply, in a way I had never seen before. Their veneration was something that transcended anything I had known in my own life. It was quiet and deep, rooted in shared passions, and simple, effortless companionship that spoke of years of dedication.

Jeff and Muffy had met at an antique auction, a place both of them adored. He was a quirky, endearing man from Massachusetts, tall and distinguished with childlike enthusiasm for his craft. He was a master of restoring antiques—pieces of history he carefully brought back to life, polishing and reviving them with an artistry matched by few. It was a business he built for himself, but more than that, it was a work of devotion.

While his business was impressive, it was his love for Muffy that defined him. Jeff had never been married before. Muffy, fierce, brilliant woman she was, had found a peace with him she'd never known in earlier years. They spent eight beautiful years together, filled with calm nights talking of things they loved, sharing stories

NEW LIFE, A NEW MENU

over dinners, and attending auctions where they both got lost in the history and beauty of forgotten treasures. They were inseparable partners, and despite Muffy's deteriorating health, Jeff stood by her side, unwavering.

When Muffy's time came, it was Jeff who held her hand. It was Jeff who made sure she was never alone. I wasn't there to witness it, to see the tenderness of their final moments together, but I didn't need to be. I knew, with every fiber of my being, that Muffy was in good hands. Jeff, whose love for her had been unshakable, transformed into an unyielding source of strength. He was her rock in those final days, the one person who offered her the peace she needed as she slipped away. As I struggled with my own emotions—guilt for not being there, grief for the loss of the woman who was my second mother—I found solace in knowing Jeff was there. He was the steady hand that guided her through the most difficult journey of all.

I think back on those days with a sense of regret and deep sorrow. I wish I had been there more for Muffy. I wish I had taken the time to visit her, to sit with her, to tell her what she meant to me before it was too late, but life has a way of moving too fast, pulling us in a million directions, and I allowed myself to be engulfed by the frenzy. I thought I could keep running—if I kept pushing forward and meeting the demands of work and family, I would somehow find balance.

I sat in the quiet after her passing, realizing that balance had never been the point. What I neglected, what I had failed to see, was the need for presence—not in my work, but in my relationships, in the moments that irrefutably mattered.

In the aftermath of Muffy's passing, it was Jeff who became my guardian angel. In a way, he became a new family member to me. He had lost the treasured person of his life, yet, through his pain, he offered me unconditional support. He was there, not with advice or words of wisdom but with patient empathy. His presence became a source of stability in my own life—a reminder that even in the face of the hardest losses, there was room for affinity, for connection, for new beginnings.

I leaned on Jeff in those months that followed. His steady friendship and fatherly affection helped me navigate my own grief and the chaos of my life. In a strange way, he stepped into the role of a protector in a way I never expected. He watched over me as I struggled with the weight of my own decisions, as I pushed myself through the motions of life, never fully stopping to reflect on what I was running from.

As much as I leaned on Jeff, I knew nothing could replace Muffy's loss. She had been a lighthouse for me, guiding me through the darkest moments of my life, and her absence left a void I didn't know how to fill. Yet, in Jeff's gracious presence, I found a thread of continuity—a reminder that love, even after loss, endures. He had witnessed Muffy's strength and grace in her final days, and it was through him I learned the true depth of her endearment and the legacy she left behind.

Muffy's death marked the end of one chapter, but Jeff's steadfast support guided me through the next. Even in the most heart-wrenching moments of my life, I knew I wasn't alone. The bond that formed between Muffy, Jeff, and me was a testament to the enduring power of love—a love that transcended time, space, and even death itself. In that love, I found a way to heal, to move forward, and to make sense of the chaos that had come to define my life.

CHAPTER 24

The Phantom of Fulfillment

After Muffy's passing, the weight of grief settled into the muffled corners of my heart, and in a desperate attempt to keep moving, I threw myself into my work. The pain of losing her was unbearable, but I couldn't allow myself to linger in it—not when there was so much to prove, to accomplish. The transition from Salamander Hotels to a larger corporation had offered the promise of something greater, a fresh start I hoped would allow me to leave behind the fragments of my past. An iconic new hotel in St. Petersburg, Florida, with storied history and grandeur, seemed like the perfect stage for this next act.

I stepped into the vast Mediterranean-inspired structure with iron railings and cypress beams that whispered stories of a time long past. There was something regal about it, a place that offered both history and possibility. I was ready for this new challenge, ready to take the helm as director of restaurant operations, overseeing six outlets and tasked with transforming them into something exceptional. I threw myself into this role, driven by the hope that achieving success in this new setting would bring fulfillment.

As the weeks wore on, something shifted. The excitement I once felt began to blur. The external markers of success—accolades, projects completed, and high-profile events—seemed increasingly hollow. I was successful, yes, but I was also losing sight of the deeper purpose behind it all.

Matt, the chef who led the culinary team, became a central figure in this shift. He was a big man with an even bigger presence, but his leadership was subtle in the best possible way. Matt wasn't the typical arrogant chef who demanded respect simply through his title. He earned it through his actions, through his willingness to work beside his team in the trenches, whether it was during busy shifts or late-night event prep. His Midwestern roots showed in his work ethic: driven, grounded, and steady.

We quickly became partners in the food and beverage operations, collaborating on everything from menu design to high-profile events. Together, we planned bold activations—like Yelloween, a gala that blended elegance with a touch of mischief—and curated the summer concert series, which became a signature event for the hotel. Through it all, I admired Matt not for his culinary prowess but for his ability to find joy in the work. His passion was contagious, and it was easy to get swept up in the excitement of our creative endeavors.

While Matt grounded me in the work itself, there was another influence at the Iconic Hotel who was shaping my professional growth: Barb, the general manager. Barb had said something during my interview that stuck with me: "Sometimes you have to take a left turn." At the time, I'd heard those words as an invitation—an opportunity to chart a new course, to discover something deeper.

Barb was a force in her own right—calm, unwavering, and always in control. She carried herself with an understated authority that commanded respect without needing to demand it. I watched her from the periphery, noted how she managed her responsibilities with grace and unshakable focus. She embodied poise, effortlessly managing the entire operation. In quiet, reflective moments, I pondered whether I could ever achieve Barb's balance, composure, and decisiveness. Her ability to manage the weight of large corporate structure and still nurture the individual components of the business, was something I longed to emulate.

• NEW LIFE, A NEW MENU •

I also found myself questioning the path I had chosen. Could I lead like Barb, with such steadfast control, and still manage the parts of my life that mattered beyond work? Was it possible to "take the left turn" into success without losing sight of the other pieces of my soul—like my relationship with my son, or the emotional wounds I had yet to face from Muffy's death?

During this time of questioning and quiet transformation, there was another key figure who helped shape the leader I was becoming: Viviana, the director of HR. From the very beginning, she took me under her wing—patiently showing me the ropes, extending grace when I faltered, and offering support when I needed it most. Viviana brought a deep well of maturity and experience to her role, and she didn't simply mentor me in process or policy, she modeled humanity in leadership. Through her, I understood that success wasn't measured by performance metrics or project wins—it was measured by how you treat people, especially in moments of stress and uncertainty. She softened the edges of my leadership style, helping me carry strength with compassion, and gave me confidence to ascend into the complex world of a large corporation with both competence and heart.

At the same time, I met Veronica, another leader who would come to play an important role in my life. Veronica was intelligent, quick-witted, and as equally driven as I was. She had a contagious energy about her. At first, our conversations were about the day-to-day operations at work, the challenges, and the victories we shared. Slowly, I saw something more in Veronica—an understanding of the internal struggles that accompanied professional ambition. She wasn't another corporate player, she was someone who, like me, was grappling with balancing external success with internal fulfillment. In her, I saw a reflection of my own ambitions and conflicts.

What intrigued me most was the way she had found balance—a way of pushing forward in her career while holding on to what mattered outside of work. We didn't become close overnight, but there was a kinship that slowly formed between us, one rooted in our shared understanding of the pressure and sacrifice inherent in corporate life. Veronica would later become someone who helped me navigate the path ahead, but in these early days, she was a symbol of something I was yearning for—an embodiment of what was possible if I learned to balance work and life.

Then, the 2020 pandemic arrived—a force that nobody could have foreseen, yet one that, in its wake, forced us all to confront the fragility of everything. The world, as I knew it, crumbled. Layoffs hit our company hard, and with them came the unsettling realization that even the most carefully crafted career could be dismantled in an instant.

The external world changed rapidly, and it forced me to ask questions I had long avoided. Was my work worth it if the foundation beneath it collapsed so easily?

The truth I had been avoiding became impossible to ignore. My work, my success—it had never been enough. I had chased after recognition, after achievement, after the illusion of fulfillment, but in doing so, I neglected the very things that should have mattered most. This unprecedented crisis forced me to confront the emptiness I was ignoring. True healing, true fulfillment, would have to come from within.

CHAPTER 25

The Illusion of Stillness

The world slowed, then stopped, and with it, a part of me stopped too. As businesses shuttered and the once-bustling streets became eerily subdued, the reality of an uncertain future settled heavily upon me. The pandemic, like a vast and invisible storm, swept through everything I had built, leaving in its wake an unsettling calm. My industry, the one that consumed my life, stood still, and with it, so did I. Overnight, the drone of activity, pressures, and demands vanished, leaving only silence. The silence was both deafening and suffocating. In this stillness, I had taken volunteer furlough, seeking to create space for something new. The opportunity to step away from my relentless work seemed like a gift, an invitation to reconnect with myself, to find a semblance of balance between work and home life that I had long denied myself.

At first, I tried to embrace this newfound freedom, burying myself in the routines of home life—cooking for the family, walking the dogs, tackling the endless loop of household chores. Virtual school became a strange new reality, one in which I struggled to keep up, not only with the logistics of remote learning but with the mounting feeling of being lost.

I should have felt grateful. I should have felt lucky. Our beautiful home, the spacious two-story house with its pool, the quiet, affluent neighborhood we lived in—it all seemed so perfect on the surface, a life some dreamed of. I should have been content.

At times, I was. In my still moments—during my walks, in the space between tasks—I acknowledged the beauty of it. Yet the quiet emptiness under the surface remained. I was adrift. The absence of my work left a void I didn't know how to fill. My days blurred, an endless series of tasks with no real sense of accomplishment or purpose. I was physically present with my family, but emotionally I was somewhere else, somewhere I couldn't quite reach.

The world around me was uncertain, fractured by fear and isolation. The industry I dedicated my life to was in ruins, and I could not escape the despair of seeing many friends and colleagues face unimaginable losses. The reality of it settled in my chest, a constant ache. Yet, there I was—safe, sheltered, with everything I needed. How could I reconcile this guilt? How could I justify feeling unsettled, even while others struggled?

Days passed in a blur. I buried myself in my MBA courses, in books, in the constant pursuit of something that might offer meaning. I pushed myself to learn, to grow, to be grateful, but nothing stuck. The endless cycle of trying to better myself only highlighted the absence of something deeper, something essential I had neglected for years. Without the structure of my career, I had no frame of reference for who I was outside of work. I had no external validation or a measure of success. All I heard was the echo of silence. My partner and I were both working from home now, though my role was drastically different. While we were together, the proximity only revealed the distance between us.

There were moments of connection, of shared laughter, but they were fleeting, too often overtaken by the tension that lingered beneath the surface. Our relationship was heavily burdened as we struggled to balance the demands of a world that had completely changed. Yet, in the chaos and uncertainty of the pandemic, I found something unexpected—a chance to reconnect with my children, to slow down and be present in a way I hadn't before.

Every morning, we would gather for PE with Joe, the online workout sessions that became our family ritual. We laughed together, trying to keep up with the energetic routines, and on Fridays, we dressed up in costumes, embracing the absurdity and joy of it all. These moments of levity were a bright spot in an otherwise heavy time, something I remember often now. We would walk the neighborhood, admiring the trees and flowers, feeling the warmth of the sun on our skin. We swam in the pool, playing together in the water, savoring the simplicity of these moments.

Then, one afternoon, everything changed. We lived in a gated community with a constant security presence—a place that was supposed to feel safe, almost impenetrable. Yet, it was one of the community's own security vehicles that brought my older son home, his wrists shattered, blood dripping from his knees. My son, who had recently gotten into the best shape of his life, had fallen off his bike, braking both wrists.

The image of him, blood dripping from his knees, his wrists broken, is seared in my memory. The accident was a vicious stroke of destiny. He had been so proud of his progress, of the strength he had built over the past few months, and now he was in excruciating pain, unable to do anything for himself.

During this time, I undeniably bonded with him. As he recovered from multiple surgeries, I became his caregiver, helping him with everything—from getting to the bathroom to showering. He was tall, and I had to stand on a ladder to wash his hair, a moment that brought many laughs between us despite the seriousness of the situation. It was a bittersweet bonding experience, one that felt like it made up for lost time. I thought of the birthdays, the holidays, and the years when I hadn't been fully present.

My older son came into my life when he was three, and though I always loved him as my own, there were gaps that had never been filled. In this moment, the walls came down. We shared something raw and unspoken, a connection born from pain, vulnerability, and time spent together.

With my younger son, I tried to be more present. We read books together before bed and went on walks, and I worked hard to create memories he would carry with him. His bond with me was different—there were no years of missed time, no distance. I cherished our moments, our subdued routines, knowing that the bond between us was strong, even if I hadn't always been the parent I wanted to be, I was his mom. Despite the challenges, I tried to give him what I had denied him before—my full attention, my genuine presence, my time. I wasn't perfect, but I was here now, trying, really trying.

The pandemic brought everything to a head, stripping away the distractions and forcing me to confront the gaps in my life, both the ones that existed within myself and the ones I had unknowingly left between me and the people I loved so much. The irony was not lost on me: I was living in a house filled with everything I wanted, surrounded by people who loved me, yet I still felt lost. The stillness, the isolation, the endless loop of daily life—it was all a reflection of something deeper.

This was a period of introspection and discomfort, as I grappled with aspects of my life that didn't align with my expectations. The days blended—one indistinguishable from the next, a monotonous cycle. I sought distraction in small tasks, yet none of them filled the cavernous void that had opened within me. The absence of work, the lack of a driving purpose, became a silent, insidious force. It scraped at me in the quiet moments, a haunting realization that, without the identity I meticulously constructed, I was unmoored.

What was I now? Who was I without my career, without the challenges, the victories, the constant push forward?

I couldn't shake the feeling that I had lost a part of myself, a piece of me buried somewhere in the weight of my accomplishments and the relentless pursuit of success. My innate Russian soul, heavy with the sense of duty and survival instilled in me from childhood, longed for something more soul-stirring, more meaningful. There was an ache, a hollowness no amount of work, no external success, could satisfy. I was suspended in the delicate balance of family life, trying desperately to internalize it, in the closed loop of chores and binge-watching TV.

My mother's voice reverberated in my thoughts, a reminder of the tenets by which I had lived my life for so long. She often spoke of sacrifice, of the relentless pursuit of what you never fully reached—always pushing ahead, always striving. Now, as I spent my days walking the streets of our neighborhood, cooking family meals, and attempting to rebuild connections fractured over time, I found myself questioning everything I thought I knew about fulfillment. I tried. I truly did.

The first holidays felt like a fleeting reprieve from the relentless storm in my chest. There were moments of joy—small victories, like watching my son's face light up as he unwrapped gifts or the warmth of a homemade meal shared around the table. They were never enough. The joy was tinged with a sense of guilt that settled deep within. I wasn't bringing in an income, I wasn't contributing to the larger world in a way that mattered. My soul, accustomed to the beats of professional life, now faced an emptiness that felt alien and suffocating. The fear of being irrelevant—fading into nothingness—lingered at the edges of every thought, every moment of stillness. In the silence of those long hours, I wondered if I was failing as a mother, as a partner. Perhaps, in the pursuit of my career, I had neglected the very foundation of who I was meant to be.

In my confusion, I continued to search. My walks with my younger son became both an escape and a self-discovery. As we wandered the streets, I reflected on my own journey and my relationship with him. There was a sweetness to our time together, a bond that, despite my absence in the early years of his life, never wavered.

With my older son, however, the pain of lost time weighed heavily. I had missed so much of his life, and although we now shared precious moments—his smile as he slowly healed, our shared laughter as I helped him with the simplest tasks—there was a distance between us that could never wholeheartedly be bridged. Although I had supported him during his recovery, I regretted not being there when he most needed me. Time had slipped away, a harsh reminder that no amount of nurturing erased the years I lost in pursuit of something I thought mattered more.

Keenly aware of the contradiction, I was desperate for connection, for meaning, yet unable to escape the very life I built in hopes of finding it. Work had always been my sanctuary, a place where I validated my identity, assessed my value, and pursued my aspirations. Now, with the industry in shambles, with no external validation to seek, I was forced to look inward. There, in the quietest moments, I met myself for the first time in a long time. I asked questions I never dared ask before.

What was I seeking? Was it really success that had driven me, or had it been something deeper, something more insidious—the fear of being forgotten, of being invisible in a world that constantly demanded more?

In the hollow ache that had grown louder with each passing day, I found myself grappling, unsure if answers would ever come. The world was in chaos, yes. The pandemic had broken things, shattered lives, and forced us all to reexamine our priorities. Yet, as I walked the path of my own internal reckoning, I couldn't ignore the disparity between those who had weathered this storm with relative ease and those who, like me, were fighting to keep afloat. Some people were on yachts, cruising the seas of privilege, while others barely managed to secure a lifejacket. Some found solace in their luxuries, their distractions, while I was standing at the edge of the abyss, searching for a thread of meaning to hold on to. I was no longer certain what I was supposed to be, who I was supposed to become.

For a considerable amount of time, I fulfilled the roles of an unwavering leader, a committed worker, a partner, and a mother, only to find myself struggling to reconstruct a life that no longer aligned with my perceived identity. The storm had taken so much from me, yet it was in the eye of that storm where I saw the contours of myself more clearly. I realized the journey I had been on—the path of constant striving—was not the only one. The illusion of fulfillment had kept me running, but now, as I stood still, as I sat in the quietude of my home, I saw the emptiness of that chase.

What did it mean to live a meaningful life? What did it mean to truly connect with those I loved, to be present, not only physically but emotionally?

The questions burrowed into my mind, relentless in their demand for answers, yet I could not bring myself to grasp solutions. There was no clear way forward. Perhaps that was the point—the truth that eluded me for so long was that fulfillment did not come from perfection or accomplishments.

So, each day became an act of discovery—an attempt to find peace amid the chaos, to give myself permission not to have all the answers, to let go of the need for control. It was in these cracks of uncertainty I felt something else—a faint sparkle of possibility.

Perhaps by surrendering the past, I created space for the future I had been too afraid to confront. I believed—no, I convinced myself—I was on the precipice of discovering something. I surrendered to the stillness of the pandemic, hoping to find myself in this silence. The weight of the world, the choices I made, and the years I lost, started to shift. There was something in that void, something I was certain would fill me if I simply waited long enough.

Like all illusions, the truth was never far behind. Reality—stubborn, relentless reality—set in. The undeniable truth was that the balance I had so desperately sought was slipping away from me.

My partner, who had long carried the burden of our family's

responsibilities, was no longer able to do so. The strain had taken its toll, and it became painfully clear I could no longer run from the responsibilities I once viewed as chains—responsibilities that now seemed like an inescapable pull toward something I couldn't resist. The luxury of staying home, of being present with my children, of striving for self-discovery and introspection, was a luxury I could no longer afford.

***

Once again, the world shifted, forcing me back into the momentum of survival. The pandemic had upended everything, but now, the market was beginning to churn again.

In Florida, the prospects were bleak—no jobs for me, no opportunities to move forward. The pull toward the next chapter was inevitable. Then, when the opportunity to move to New Orleans arose, it felt like a lifeline—another escape from the dissonance of stagnation. I had dreamed of working for the Ritz-Carlton for years, and now here it was, the chance to prove myself again. It felt like an escape from the shadows of doubt that had loomed over me, an invitation to re-enter the arena.

In the face of this seemingly perfect opportunity, there was no elation. There was only a resonant understanding of the significance of the decision I was making. I had abandoned the pursuit of self-discovery, forsaken the fragile balance I longed for, and plunged once again into the very depths of challenge that I knew all too well.

Immersion in the work—letting it engulf me and occupy my every waking thought—had become both a refuge and a prison. The mild, nagging voices of doubt and inner conflict were silenced by the ceaseless demands of the world I chose to navigate. I had mastered this art before, and now, I would master it again.

We sold the house in Florida, took that bold step toward the unknown, and settled in a modest home in a new state. We clung desperately to the hope that this relocation—this fresh start—would stabilize our finances, unlock greater opportunities for our children, and realign the compass of our lives. I accepted the physical toll of driving an hour each way to work, wearing down my body in exchange for a new beginning.

As I fought the weariness in my limbs, I found myself trapped in a familiar cycle of exhaustion and internal conflict, one I had known well, but never fully understood. New Orleans—a city of music, grit, and chaos—presented a market unlike any I had encountered before. The scars of a pandemic were still fresh, and reopening operations in the aftermath of its devastation felt Sisyphean. The city's harsh restrictions, mask mandates, and capacity limitations, all while serving weary, anxious, disoriented clientele, pushed me to the very edge of my endurance. Each day felt like a test of both physical and emotional stamina.

I worked hours stretching from dawn to dusk, to the very brink of collapse. The validation I sought—fleeting and elusive—became the lifeline that prevented me from sinking into an emotional abyss. I leaned into the exhaustion as if it somehow absolved me, finding a strange solace in the relentless pulse of struggle. In the turbulence of New Orleans, I was not alone.

The presence of individuals who embodied the very spirit of the city sustained me. Among them was Tammy, whose instincts were as deep and rooted in the city as the oak trees lining the streets of the French Quarter. A native of New Orleans, Tammy was not just another worker; she was the heartbeat of the operation, someone whose experience in the world of hospitality had been honed in the crucible of New Orleans itself.

As a former general manager of a family-owned restaurant, Tammy embodied an elegance in the execution of her duties and possessed an intuitive understanding of the intricacies of service. She was never a mere employee; she was a force, an indomitable spirit. I felt the authenticity in her approach to service—a rare quality that transcended professionalism and entered the realm of true care. Tammy kept me tethered to the reality of the business, offering wisdom drawn from the depths of her own vast experience. Her unwavering support and adept handling of the often-turbulent dynamics enabled me to establish an A-team in an environment where turnover was a common occurrence.

We were alike in many ways, but also strikingly different in our temperaments, and it was precisely this difference that made her presence so invaluable. Her humor, her laughter, and her unfailing resilience turned the most grueling days—such as those interminable high teas during the holidays or the madness of gingerbread-house-building events—into moments of shared camaraderie. In her, I found not only a colleague but a friend, and in the end, she kept me organized, kept me motivated, and, above all, reminded me that it was possible to find joy even amid the madness.

Then there was Ann Marie, who, like Tammy, was a steady presence in the swirling storm. Calm, composed, and supremely competent, Ann Marie was the anchor on the floor—the one who ensured all the moving parts fell into place, seamlessly and without fanfare. Yet her most distinguishing quality was her sincerity. Ann Marie was not merely performing her duties, she genuinely cared. I would watch her move through the space, engaging with guests not out of obligation but with a warmth and attentiveness that spoke of a deep, intrinsic understanding of the human condition. In her, I saw the embodiment of hospitality in its truest form—not the act of serving but the deep-rooted and unspoken connection that service can create between one person and another. The guests felt it, and so did the team. Ann Marie's calming presence, her ability to listen and respond to the unspoken needs of both guests and staff, was a quality that made her indispensable.

We, too, shared a sense of humor that allowed us to manage the pressure weighing so heavily upon us, as all three of us battled the chaos with the kind of lightness that only those who have wholeheartedly embraced the madness can understand. Together, these women—Tammy and Ann Marie—formed the backbone of our success, and in their own ways, they embodied the essence of what it meant to be a New Orleanian. They were not alone in this.

There were others—many others—who, each in their own unique way, gave me glimpses of what true management really was. Jason, the bartender, became as familiar to the guests as the hotel's architecture, his understated competence and ready smile providing solace to many. Despite his unassuming presence, his service was characterized by a depth, calmness, and reliability that ensured everything ran smoothly. Jeremy, the resident musician, was one of the finest trumpet players in the United States. His melodies would float through the air, soothing frayed nerves, inviting people to pause, reflect, and connect. Jeremy, too, embodied the spirit of the city—a city whose people, in their unwavering concern for others, create an atmosphere of warmth, where hospitality is not merely a transaction but an act of care, of understanding.

Then there was Myles—larger than life, a true New Orleans native, and the epitome of the city's indomitable spirit. Myles was a perpetual optimist whose boundless energy and unwavering positivity provided a steady sense of hope. He wasn't only optimistic—he had a way of making you believe that joy, no matter how fleeting, was always worth seeking. In moments when everything around me felt uncertain, his ability to laugh off the smallest frustrations made me question my own habit of clinging to seriousness. His perspective instilled in me the understanding that not every battle required intensity.

Myles saw the world as one of endless possibility, and no matter how daunting the task, he framed it in a light that made us believe there was always a way forward. His laughter, his warmth, and his sheer joy for life were infectious. More than a colleague, Myles was an irresistible force, lighting up even the darkest days with his optimism.

In New Orleans, at the Ritz-Carlton, I found something remarkable—a deeper understanding of the essence of the city. It was in the people—the interactions, the way each individual brought their unique energy to the collective spirit of the hotel. The city, like the hotel, thrived not on the superficial gestures of service but on the genuine care and connection that radiated from its inhabitants. They reminded me, over and over again, that care was not about grand gestures but about the subtle, often invisible threads that bind us all in a shared humanity.

There were days, yes, when the weight was too much to bear. I would drive home in the late hours, barely able to keep my eyes open, fighting against the unrelenting pull of sleep. My only comfort was the phone call to my mother. In the early morning hours in Russia, she would answer. Her voice, steady and grounding, kept me tethered to something outside the madness. I would arrive home, drained and battered, and throw my body into the bath, hoping to soak away the fatigue, only to rise again in a few hours to repeat it all. Yet, in this never-ending cycle, I found something—validation, yes, but something more—a fleeting sense of purpose.

The work became my refuge, my escape from the void I once sought to understand. For a brief moment, I felt as though I was turning the corner. I was becoming the person I wished to be—more present, more successful, more connected to the world. The strain of the pandemic, the exhaustion of those early months, forged me into something more resilient, more capable. All that—every ounce of progress—was erased in a single moment.

A category five hurricane—one of the most devastating storms to hit the region—swept through New Orleans, ripping apart our neighborhood. The damage to our home was significant; the insurance covered only a fraction of the cost. We found ourselves drained, financially and emotionally, sinking deeper into the mire of uncertainty. The façade of stability I had worked so hard to create cracked, and in its place, a new struggle emerged.

NEW LIFE, A NEW MENU

In the middle of the devastation, when it seemed that everything was slipping away from me, a call arrived—a lifeline, yes, but also a reminder of everything I attempted to leave behind.

It was Hayato, my former mentor, reaching out with an offer to return to the world I knew intimately: the director of food and beverage position at the Omni Charlotte. The salary was significantly higher than what I earned in New Orleans, and it offered a path forward for my family—a way to climb out of the financial hole we had dug.

On the surface, it was everything I had wanted: security, opportunity, a chance to step back into the professional world with authority. Yet, beneath that, there was a sense of unease—a voice whispering that perhaps this was not the escape I hoped for, but simply a return to the forces that had kept me in perpetual motion.

We moved quickly, driven by a sense of urgency, as if to outrun the heaviness of the past. I couldn't quite tell if we were running toward something better or simply running from what we left behind. Our fourth move in as many years felt like a desperate attempt to shake off the fatigue and exhaustion that had seeped into every corner of our lives. North Carolina promised a quieter pace and a fresh start, and I convinced myself this time, it would be different.

The house we found was beautiful, nestled in a town that seemed removed from the noise, where the flow of life felt slower, more deliberate. For a moment, I allowed myself to believe that perhaps this was the answer I was searching for. Even as I tried to breathe easier in this new space, the undercurrent of doubt never truly left. The exhaustion I had carried from New Orleans, the emotional toll of constantly uprooting and trying to reinvent myself, was not something a new address erased.

Despite all my efforts to carve out something new and more balanced, the weight of my decision lingered. Returning to the demands of work I thought I left behind, was a heavy realization. It was a step back into a life of constant striving, a life where my worth was measured by professional success and where the need for control and achievement often drowned out the simpler, quieter things. The storm I weathered in New Orleans—long hours, relentless push for perfection—followed me. As I settled into my new role, I felt the disquiet of knowing that no matter how many times I moved, no matter how many times I tried to escape, I could not outrun the cycle of work that had become my life.

CHAPTER 26

The Mirage of Success

Charlotte, North Carolina. The name alone brought with it the promise of a fresh start, the prospect of a new chapter, the allure of a title that gleamed like a beacon—a validation, an accomplishment I had earned. The executive position at Omni was, on the surface, the culmination of years of relentless toil. It was the recognition I had craved, the opportunity to lead, to shape a legacy, to rise above the tumult of the world that unraveled in the wake of the pandemic.

Yet, as I stood in the grand foyer of our new home in Gastonia, the scent of fresh paint lingering in the air, I could not shake a sensation of unease. This should have been it. The reward for my struggle. The triumph of ambition realized. I had the beautiful house, the status, and the recognition, but somewhere, buried beneath the polished floors and carefully manicured lawns, something was missing. I could not pinpoint it, but I knew it was there. An inescapable emptiness, a question unanswered.

The industry, with its melody and pulse, had always been a part of me. It encompassed the art of connection and the delicate balance between service and personal touch. The pride I felt in the work—the thrill of creating unforgettable experiences, of welcoming people, of orchestrating moments that would stay with them long after they checked out—remained steadfast within me. It was not that I had fallen out of ardor with my career. In many ways, love remained radiant. What had shifted was the impossibility of balancing it all—the endless demands of my job with the deep, aching need to be present for my family, to nurture the relationships long neglected. Work was still my escape, my anchor, my refuge.

The days were long, the tasks unceasing. Reopening the hotel after the pandemic was grueling, the weight of it pressing down on all of us. In those early months, I had found meaning. I was doing what I loved. I was part of a team again, working together, problem-solving, and finding ways to connect in a rapidly changing world.

But as the days turned into months, the realization settled in: the more I succeeded in my career, the more I lost touch with my family, my relationship, and my inner peace. The hotel was my world; the people I served and led were mine, but in that world, there was little room for anything else. I had given everything to it, convinced that one more achievement, one more success, one more accomplishment would be the key to making everything whole.

I did not resent my work. I never could. The magic of hospitality had shaped me, molded me. It was deeply ingrained in my being, manifesting in the way I welcomed guests, the joy I felt when my team achieved success, and the exhilaration of realizing a concept. Yet the pursuit of this success had come at a cost that I had not fully understood before.

I looked at my partner and children with an ache. I succeeded at work, but I failed to show up for them. There were moments of connection, moments of warmth, but they were fleeting, overshadowed by the weight of my constant drive for more. The house in Gastonia, with its two stories and manicured lawn, stood as a symbol of my triumph but also a reminder that life was still unbalanced. On paper, I had everything—the home, the career, the recognition—but the peace I hoped for, the contentment I longed for, continued to elude me.

My partner and I, too, had found new ways to communicate and connect. There were moments of joy and closeness that made me believe we were healing. Yet, I could not help but feel that the real work—the hardest work—was ahead of me.

Could I find peace in this life I had created, or was I doomed to chase the next thing forever, never quite satisfied with what I had?

The house—which should have been a symbol of all I worked for—was a reflection of my inner turmoil. On the outside, it was the epitome of success— the American dream, the achievement. Inside, restless, still yearning for something more.

The passion I had for my work had not faded. It was there, woven into the fabric of who I was. However, I could no longer ignore the truth that my relentless pursuit of success had left me adrift in my own life. I could no longer deny that the balance I desperately sought remained out of reach. In my work, I had found purpose. In my family, I had found endearment. To reconcile the two—to make them coexist in harmony—was a challenge I had yet to master. So, I continued to struggle—to search, to reach for something that I was unsure even existed. The journey was far from over.

***

Jeremy entered the picture like a breath of fresh air. Ten years my junior, a man of Spanish descent with ambition coursing through his veins, he was everything I was not—at least on the surface. He was the embodiment of youthful energy, brimming with a contagious confidence that somehow filled the rooms we worked in. His charm was undeniable, his presence magnetic. He had the ability to instill confidence in you, even in the face of seemingly insurmountable challenges. Sweet, strong, and relentlessly charismatic, Jeremy was a natural leader in his own right.

My new partner in crime, he was a kindred spirit in many ways. Together, we achieved new milestones, pushed boundaries, and created something that felt bigger than both of us. We worked tirelessly—nights spent refining guest satisfaction scores, brainstorming ideas to elevate the service, and creating experiences that would stay with our guests long after they left. He had a unique ability to enhance my authentic self, embracing the crazy, fun, and slightly unorthodox side of me that had become my trademark over the years.

My journey had shaped me into someone who knew how to make people smile and how to engage guests and staff alike with irrepressible warmth. Through all the people I had encountered along the way, I had learned how to be a force of positive energy, the eternal optimist in the room, even when it felt like my own life was in turmoil.

I often wondered: was this genuinely who I was? Or had it become a façade I wore to shield myself from the deeper questions? The champion of positivity, the perpetually smiling face, the one who made everyone feel seen and heard—had that become my mask? Was I hiding behind it, too afraid to confront the parts of me that felt lost, the parts of me that longed for something more than accolades and success?

I got to discover the answer to this question a year later.

Jeremy and I were in sync, creatively and professionally. He brought a sense of youthful enthusiasm that complemented my seasoned experience. I watched him handle the team with a mix of confidence and kindness that, while perhaps different from my style, still resonated with me. We made a formidable duo, pushing ourselves and our team to new heights.

Omni was no different from the other places I'd worked before—it was a new opportunity, a new challenge, a new chapter that called for innovation, for transformation, for something special. That is exactly what I intended to create, but the work was not as easy as it seemed. The stakes were high; the expectations never relented. We consistently strived for excellence, for improvement, and we consistently sought to stay at the forefront of our industry. We were being judged not simply by the company but by every guest that walked through the doors. Every interaction counted. Every detail mattered.

Despite the unyielding pressure, I worked diligently, as I had always done. The expectations were overwhelming, but in the intensity, I found a strange comfort. Perhaps it was the familiar cadence of the industry—the adrenaline of the daily grind, the challenge of making everything work seamlessly. My work had become a source of both escape and validation. Here, in the hustle of the hotel, amid the never-ending cycle of service, I was able to momentarily forget the other parts of my life that felt so unresolved.

Still, I had found a new syncopation, a new partnership in Jeremy, yet the duality of my existence—the constant tension between the person I wanted to be at work and the person I longed to be at home—remained. In the echo of my successes, in the middle of all the energy I poured into creating a meaningful experience for guests, was this the life I wanted? Could I continue to sustain this pace, this constant striving for more, or was I simply running from something deeper, something I was afraid to face?

***

One day, the call came for me to return to the hotel in St. Petersburg, this time as the director of food and beverage. The resort, once my sanctuary and my battleground, was undergoing a grand transformation, and they had invited me to be part of it. The weight of that call struck me with an unsettling intensity—an offer that sounded both familiar and thrilling. It was as if a door I closed years ago had swung, beckoning me back into a world I had always loved. A world that, despite its challenges, had always felt like home.

The Iconic Hotel, Florida—this place I once poured myself into—was now offering me another chance. Another stage to display my craft, to build something anew. It promised grandeur, a title that elevated me further, back to the place where I felt my professional roots were planted, where my network, my old friends, and my comfort lay in waiting. How could I resist?

It felt like fate, but this time, it was different. I was not a naïve dreamer; I had built a life since then—one that required careful consideration. Yet, despite this newfound wisdom, I pushed for us to move, once again abandoning the semblance of stability we had begun to form. At this moment, my ambition overshadowed the quiet realization that something was lacking, something I was unable to reconcile within myself. I told myself it was the right thing to do—the next step, the next chapter. How could I have known, in that instant, that I was walking headlong into a choice that would ripple through the core of my existence in ways I did not yet understand?

I had recently graduated with my MBA from USF, a moment of personal pride and accomplishment. The ceremony, attended by Barb and Viviana, was meant to be a celebration of that triumph. Yet, in the accolades, the proud moments, and the joy of completing this monumental step, I found myself faced with a question that carried an unspoken weight: should I walk away from all I had achieved and step into a new challenge? A challenge I long dreamed of but that held its own set of unknowns?

The decision to go to the interview felt inevitable. The allure of the hotel was too strong. It was an opportunity to return to the spotlight, to reclaim the title I had once worn with pride, to return to a place that held meaning in my journey. Barb, the mentor who taught me that leadership was about heart and humanity as well as strategy and execution, was gone, now headed for a new beautiful resort. The hotel had a new chief, someone I knew little about. Matt had also moved to a different property to take on the role of executive chef in Tampa. The landscape had shifted—what was familiar was now shrouded in change—but there was a pull, something magnetic that urged me to step forward, to go through that door one last time.

So, with a familiar sense of resolve, I walked into the interview. I was offered the position, and it felt like the culmination of everything I had worked toward. I felt victorious, validated in the pursuit of my dreams. However, a rift opened within me. I had attained the very thing I wanted—an esteemed title, a familiar path, the return to comfort and recognition. As I stood there, basking in that fleeting moment of success, an eroding unease crept into the corners of my mind.

Was this truly what I had been searching for all along? Was I simply running away from the deeper work that I had yet to confront?

As I stood at the precipice of this decision, I felt the weight of the years—hours of work, the relentless pursuit of the next big achievement, the escape into professional glory—all crashed into me with brutal honesty. What was I really chasing? Success, yes—but success at what cost? Did I have the courage to confront the void that persisted, no matter how many accolades I piled upon myself? Would this return to the Iconic Hotel fix the things that had remained broken? Would this new opportunity provide the fulfillment I craved, or would it be yet another way to run from the deeper questions plaguing my soul?

The excitement of the offer—the familiar pull of the Iconic Hotel, the promise of renewed success—was intoxicating. This decision, this choice to take the job, was not made in a vacuum. It was laden with echoes of everything I had done before—every decision that brought me to this point.

I believed that returning to the Iconic Hotel would be a return to comfort, to familiarity, to a version of myself that I thought I knew. I did not realize that this choice would plunge me deeper into the labyrinth I was trying to escape for so long. It would be the beginning of a new chapter—one that would force me to confront the duality of my desires: the pull of ambition, the hunger for recognition, the need to prove myself, versus the quiet yearning for peace, for balance, for fulfillment not tied to what I did, but to who I was.

So, with excitement and trepidation coiled together, I walked through that door—only to find, once again, that the journey was far from over. The very thing I had been chasing—success, recognition, validation—was no longer enough to fill the silence inside me.

CHAPTER 27

The Collapse of Certainty

I arrived at the Iconic Hotel on January 9, a day etched into the timeline of my life, though it felt less like a beginning and more like stepping into the echo of something already lost. The excitement I should have felt was replaced with a creeping unease—like entering a room vacated by some truth too large to name. The silence hummed with anticipation, but not the joyful kind. I told myself it was nerves. But deep down, I knew.

The pre-opening frenzy gave me purpose, or at least a distraction. I threw myself into the work, convinced that momentum substituted for clarity. Instead of building something fresh, it felt like salvaging the remnants of a dream. The blueprint had shifted, but no one had updated the plan. Pieces were missing. The image on the box no longer matched the puzzle in our hands.

Still, I had Veronica.

She was my constant—sharp, steady, unshaken. We had worked together for years, forged through fire and impossibilities, but this felt different. The stakes were higher, the fractures deeper. On days when I doubted everything—my place, my ability, my worth—her voice tethered me back to reason.

"You're allowed to doubt," she said once, as I spiraled in the face of another impossible deadline. "But don't live there. It doesn't have to be perfect—it has to be real."

In those words, I felt the truth I had forgotten: Perfection is a moving target, and progress often begins in the rubble.

Beneath the surface of all that construction, my personal life was falling apart. In February, the call came. The one I both feared and expected. My marriage—already frayed—was over. The finality of it didn't come with shouting or drama, but with the quiet resignation of something long decayed. I told myself it wasn't over. I could fix it. This was a phase. But the knowing had already settled deep in my bones.

I was living in a hotel room, performing elegance by day, grieving in silence by night. My children were hundreds of miles away, their absence pressing against my chest like a stone I couldn't dislodge. Still, I worked. Hospitality doesn't pause for heartbreak.

At the hotel, the pace was relentless. The GM—already in place when I arrived—was poised, methodical, and respected. She had a command of process, a firm grip on results. Her version of leadership was one of precision and detachment. It wasn't cruel—it was simply devoid of the softness I had built my career around. Where I led with empathy, she led with distance.

I tried to adapt, to meet her where she stood, but the space between our values only widened. My voice felt quieter in rooms that once amplified it. I questioned everything. Was my way outdated? Had the rules changed while I wasn't looking?

Then our executive chef resigned, and something inside me cracked. I didn't have the luxury to mourn that loss. I stood up straighter. Worked longer. Whispered mantras like prayers: You can do this. You always have. Don't fall now.

Veronica kept me going. She saw the fear I tried to mask, called it out gently but firmly. Her feedback wasn't flattery—it was accountability. She wouldn't let me disappear into self-doubt. She knew when to challenge me, when to reassure me, when to remind me who I was. Together, we pulled off the impossible: opening a signature bar and patisserie in two weeks. The paint was still drying, the layout unfamiliar. We did it. February 22. A small miracle stitched together with grit and sleepless nights.

Then came Adriana.

Where Veronica steadied, Adriana ignited. She brought a fire for excellence, a fierce attention to detail honed through her Ritz-Carlton pedigree. There was heart beneath the polish—a generosity I hadn't expected. She stayed late, worked side by side, and somewhere between checklists and tea breaks, she saw me. Not the mask. Me.

"You're brilliant," she said once, her tone direct. "Stop questioning yourself. We don't have time for that."

Her belief in me was uncompromising. With her, I started to allow imperfection. Started to believe that vulnerability wasn't a weakness—it was a window. We walked by the water after long shifts, shared cups of tea in tucked-away corners, and in those moments, I glimpsed the woman I had been before fear set in. Before I measured my worth by execution alone.

But the tremors didn't stop.

The scaffolding of my identity—my work, my titles, the vision I had held—crumbled. The image I constructed of myself no longer fit. What once felt like armor now felt like a shell. Hollow. Heavy.

Three months after that call, the divorce was final. I was no longer anyone's wife. I was a mother at a distance. The hotel, in all its grandeur and momentum, continued without pause. I showed up, even when I was unraveling. Especially then.

In that quiet unraveling, Sean reappeared—not with answers, but with presence. He didn't need me to explain. He sat with me in the grief. Sometimes, that's all we need to breathe.

The year didn't slow. We launched a high tea service, hosted VIPs, prepared for the GM conference. Time became a blur of pressure points and deadlines. A new restaurant opening came next—another labor under impossible timelines. I no longer expected ease. I hadn't stopped longing for grace.

Under the GM's rule, grace was scarce. Her methods worked. Her numbers proved it, but something vital was missing. As I watched her, a subtle reminder surfaced: this isn't who I want to become. Success shouldn't come at the expense of who I am.

Still, there were lanterns in the storm.

Richard, the resident manager, carried himself with a calm that soothed rooms. He spoke rarely, but listened deeply. He reminded me that leadership is not volume—it's resonance. Then there was Eve, our razor-sharp HR manager, who pierced through everything, including me. She made me laugh at myself when I needed it most. Her dry wit was a scalpel—cutting through illusion, revealing clarity.

In the still hours—between late-night emails and quiet walks—I asked the harder questions. Was I transforming, or merely enduring? Was I building a new self, or losing the one I had known?

In conversations with Veronica, Adriana, and Sean, a quieter voice surfaced within me. A voice less interested in applause, more drawn to peace. It didn't want answers. It wanted meaning.

Maybe this was what growth looked like—not the triumph of certainty, but the gentle collapse of illusion. The quiet undoing that comes before the becoming.

***

I drove.

Ten hours on the road each time, down the long stretch from Florida to North Carolina. I would count the miles not only in distance, but in aches. The humming of the highway filled the space where thoughts would otherwise overtake me. Every trip north was a strange mixture of anticipation and dread. I longed to see my children—to feel their arms around me, to step briefly into the life that had once been mine. Even as I approached the town we used to call home, I felt it slipping from my grasp. Someone else lived in the house now. Someone else stood in the frame of the door I once stood in. It wasn't only a home that had been left behind—it was the life I had poured myself into, absorbed into, built around.

I watched my children laugh and grow and learn without me, their lives unfolding in real time while I hovered at the edges like a ghost. I was still their mother—but from a distance. My hugs came on weekends, my reassurance in phone calls. I loved them no less, but I had become, in so many ways, less present.

There was a particular moment—standing in the foyer of the house we once shared—when the silence hit differently. It echoed. The walls no longer knew my footsteps. The air felt neutral, not warm. I realized then that I wasn't only grieving a marriage, I was grieving the vanishing of a world I had helped create.

I had not vanished. I was still here, driving, showing up, building, working, loving. That realization, quiet and stubborn, stayed with me as I made the long drive back to Florida once again. Exhausted. Hollow. Still somehow whole.

Maybe this is what growth looked like. Not a linear ascent, but a return—again and again—to the places that broke you, until you finally learn how to hold the pain without letting it define you.

Maybe, just maybe, that's where becoming begins.

CHAPTER 28

The Shattered Path Forward

The last few months felt like a blur, a disorienting tangle of moments that slipped away faster than I grasped them. Despite my intention to reconnect with my children, the trip to North Carolina turned into a confrontation with the wreckage of my life. I left thinking I was seeking solace in the familiarity of what had once been, but upon my return, I was forced to face something much harder: the realization that nothing would ever be the same. The foundation of my life, which had once seemed solid, had shattered. I, standing in the ruins, had to find a way to rebuild.

I was broken in a way I hadn't expected—disoriented, adrift in a world that no longer made sense. The life I had carefully constructed, the identity I wrapped myself in, dissolved, leaving nothing but fragments of a dream I no longer held. My marriage, my career, my sense of self—they all escaped my grasp, leaving me with the painful truth that I was no longer the person I once was.

It was like waking from a dream and realizing everything you thought was real had been a delicate illusion. The pain was debilitating, relentless in its weight. I had always believed strength meant holding everything together, pushing through, and doing whatever necessary to meet the expectations of the world around me. I was learning that sometimes strength was about breaking apart.

Accepting that the once certain and unwavering parts of yourself vanished in an instant was crucial. In that brokenness, I had to make a choice: would I let it consume me, or would I find a way to move forward?

I desperately searched for a way to cope, reading countless books on divorce, hoping one would give me the clarity I needed. None of them helped—not until I came across *The Gift* by Dr. Edith Eva Eger. It became a turning point in my healing journey, one that gave me something I had been missing: perspective.

Eger's story, her survival of the Holocaust, her ability to find peace after such unimaginable suffering, made me realize that if someone endured that and still found a way to heal, perhaps I could too. Though my struggles didn't compare to hers, the feelings of isolation, fear, and hopelessness she described were familiar. I found myself drawing correlations—drawing strength from her ability to find healing in the darkest circumstances. It was in those pages I saw a path forward, even if it was one I was still too afraid to walk fully.

The journey wasn't easy, and the book didn't provide all the answers, but it planted a seed. It taught me that my pain, though real and deep, did not have to define me forever. I saw that healing didn't erase the past, it changed the way I looked at it—finding new meaning, new strength, in the broken pieces. In Eger's words, I saw the possibility of change, the hope that I could move beyond the hurt and emerge whole again, even if it was in a new, imperfect way.

Despite everything, despite the overwhelming grief, I felt something rising within me—a desire to rebuild. The career I once relied on for stability, though full of unpredictability and chaos, became a source of comfort. I had spent so much of my life shaping myself around this unpredictable world, this ever-changing landscape, but in the face of everything else falling apart, it became the one constant thing I held on to. In that instability, I found the resilience I needed to keep going.

More than that, I found that it wasn't work that kept me tethered—it was the connections. The meaningful relationships, the unexpected moments of grace and support from those who walked beside me. These were the threads that held me together when everything else unraveled. Even in the most isolated of moments, I realized I wasn't truly alone. There was a tribe, a community, waiting for me, even if I hadn't always seen it.

In this time of deep pain and loss, I found a sense of gratitude for the people in my life who had given me the space to fall apart, who allowed me to be vulnerable. It was in these moments of rawness that I realized the true value of what I had—these bonds formed not out of perfection but out of shared struggle and understanding. The flawless image I had once tried to maintain wasn't important; it was the humanity beneath it all.

The path forward was unclear, fraught with pain, uncertainty, and fear, but the truth was undeniable: I had a choice. I could remain in the ruins, consumed by the past, or I could rebuild. I couldn't give up—not now. Not when there was still fervor to be found, nor when there was still life to be lived, even in its broken, imperfect form.

I chose to move forward. It wasn't a decision born from certainty, nor did I have any illusion of an effortless road ahead. In that moment, I understood that healing wasn't about an end point; it was about the courage to take the next step, even if it was with uncertainty in my heart. Slowly, piece by broken piece, I would rebuild, not because I had the answers but because I had the choice to keep going, and that alone was enough.

The year that ensued at the Iconic Hotel was a turbulent and transformative journey. As I immersed myself deeper in the demands of the job, there was unrelenting pressure to push forward and continue shaping the hotel into a true luxury destination. It felt like a battle against the impossible expectations of the industry, the weight of my personal history, and the part of me that still wanted to give up, but something in me refused. Something kept me pushing through, despite the exhaustion, despite the fear of what would happen if I failed.

It was a trying time—one that, in hindsight, I can reflect on as both challenging and deeply rewarding. I grew professionally in ways I hadn't anticipated. While the pressure was intense, it also shaped me into a stronger individual, equipped to tackle any challenge head-on. I made mistakes, of course—mistakes that felt catastrophic in the moment but ultimately became valuable lessons. There were days when I questioned my ability to make a difference and whether I was truly suited for this. But I learned, time and time again, that growth doesn't avoid mistakes, it learns from them and moves forward.

In those instances of growth, I realized how much impact I had on the lives of others. The connections I forged with my team, with the guests, and with the people who crossed my path were meaningful. It wasn't about luxury or perfection—it was about human connections. I was learning, shaping, and contributing, not only to the hotel's success, but to something far greater: the belief that we all, in our small ways, make the world a little better, even if it was through simple gestures of kindness, understanding, or support.

The work was consuming, though, and my personal life remained on the periphery. I only saw my children during their school breaks—moments when the gaps between us stretched further than the miles that separated us. Those moments were bittersweet. They were the goalposts, the things I looked forward to, the light at the end of a very long tunnel. Yet, when they came, I often felt I wasn't truly present for them, as I was still carrying the weight of everything else—my work, my grief, my search for meaning in a life that had been shattered. Still, I held onto the idea that these moments, though short, mattered. They were my tether to something pure, something that had the potential to heal me.

I moved out of Sean's apartment and found a new place for myself—a fresh start, though it felt anything but easy. It wasn't far from where Adriana lived, and her unwavering support continued to be a lifeline. She was more than a friend at that point; she was my constant, my confidant. No matter how exhausted or broken I felt, she would drag me out, sometimes to the most random places—to dance, to laugh, to just be. Even on the nights when I felt so low that I barely summoned the energy to get out of bed, Adriana wouldn't let me sulk. She wouldn't let me sink deeper into the sadness that threatened to swallow me whole.

So, I danced. At first, it was an act of resistance, a way to say to the universe, "I'm still here. I'm still fighting." I recorded silly dance videos—my "dance therapy," a way to force myself to find joy in a moment, even if it was fleeting. Sometimes the laughter felt hollow, but other times, it was real.

Over time it became something I looked forward to, a small victory against the despair that clung to me. It wasn't perfect, of course. There were days when the sadness was too much, when the weight of everything pressed down on me too hard. However, I came to understand that healing occurs in small, everyday moments of defiance against the darkness.

> ***Healing occurs in everyday moments of defiance against darkness.***

My work and the dance therapy became intertwined in ways I hadn't expected. The hotel provided the structure and swing, while the dancing gave me the freedom to express myself in a way I hadn't been able to in a long time. It was an odd, imperfect balance, but it was the balance I needed.

I found myself constantly reminded of what I was truly fighting for—my children. They were my compass, my reason for enduring the pain, for staying grounded when everything else was spinning out of control. I would see them during their breaks, and that thought, that feeling of being close to them, became the anchor I held on to when everything else was slipping away.

As I moved forward, I knew that I hadn't fully healed. The wounds were still fresh, raw, gnawing at me in moments when I thought I could rest. I was learning to live with them—to carry them without letting them consume me. Each day, every small step forward was a victory. I had a goal. I had a plan for the future, even if it was unclear. It was for the first time in a long while, I felt the faint stirrings of hope. It wasn't a perfect hope, but it was real. It was enough to keep me going. I hadn't arrived at the place of peace yet, and I didn't know when that moment would come.

For now, though, I was dancing. Simultaneously, I was learning to honor the fragments of myself that remained, knowing that they, too, could be beautiful in their brokenness.

CHAPTER 29

The Core of My Becoming

If I think back to the first days I found myself in this industry—those trembling, uncertain days. I remember them as if they were a past life, a distant echo of who I was. It seems absurd now, the clarity with which I recall the first spark of excitement, that infectious passion that surged through me the moment I stepped into the world of hospitality.

It was then, in those early days, I became aware of an internal compulsion, a drive to immerse myself entirely in this world. Perhaps it was more than the job—it was the notion of purpose, of meaning, of submerging myself into something greater than myself. Although I didn't realize it at the time, that initial fire continued to burn through the years, transforming into various forms and illuminating my path, burning from deep within me.

I remember the distinct sensation of entering a world where every task felt monumental, where every smile had the weight of possibility. I felt as though I was part of something vast, something much larger than the sum of its parts. There was beauty in the moments of connection—exchanges that seemed trivial on the surface but, in their essence, spoke of the fragile human bond. Every relationship and encounter served as a valuable lesson, fitting into my understanding of the universe and my role within it.

In these moments I built, bit by bit, the woman I would become, the professional who would shape this world in her image, even if, deep down, I never quite knew who that woman was. In the beginning, I was so hungry for growth—for success—for validation. The industry gave me that—at least, I thought it did. I was learning, absorbing, and constantly evolving in a way that felt like a spiritual journey. As time went on, I came to realize that professional success alone never fulfilled the hunger that raged within.

I had become a machine programmed to perform, deliver, and meet expectations. In spite of everything, no matter how much I gave, no matter how many smiles I offered or challenges I conquered, I felt an unsettling emptiness—a void the job did not fill. It wasn't until I had reached a certain point in my life, when the world I had so carefully constructed fractured, that I saw the deeper truth of it all.

The joy of hospitality and the rush of the job lay not in external victories, but in the internal process, the ability to break, falter, and rise again, reformed by the experience. The industry itself had been my crucible, my forge. It had shown me the power of vulnerability, of embracing cracks that appeared in the armor, and of understanding that each fragment that fell away left space for something new to grow. The question, *Who am I, really?* had been lingering on the periphery of my mind for so long, waiting for me to come face-to-face with it. That question had no simple answer, of course. No neat conclusion to reach, no destination to arrive at. I came to understand—slowly, painfully—that perhaps we are never meant to fully answer that question. Perhaps that is the essence of being human: to exist in the state of becoming, of evolving, without ever truly arriving.

There is a certain existential weight to that realization, one I'm sure many feel in their own way. It's the weight of knowing we are both the architects and the wreckage of our lives. In seeking to define ourselves, we often find ourselves slipping into paradoxes and contradictions. The idea of "self" is ever-shifting, ever-elusive, like a figure glimpsed in a fog. In spite of everything, in the fragments of understanding we are able to seize, we are closer to who we are than we could ever be in our striving.

The truth about it—the hard truth that I had to come to terms with—is that nothing in this life is perfect. No job, no relationship, no self. There is no ultimate destination, no state of arrival, yet it is in the striving—the reaching for something better, something truer—that we find meaning.

I look back on the beginning of my career, and I realize that, in many ways, it was not the success or the accolades that shaped me—it was the constant dance of progress and failure, the ebb and flow of growth that mirrored my own internal journey. It was only through the cracks in my professional and personal life, the moments when I could not hold it together any longer, that I saw the beauty of the process.

We are not meant to become whole in one swift motion but to come undone, piece by piece, and then, over time, to rebuild ourselves in a new form. There is bounty in that brokenness, a depth that cannot be discovered through the pursuit of perfection. It is in the act of choosing to fall apart, of allowing ourselves to be vulnerable, that we find the greatest opportunities for growth.

I often reflect on my Russian heritage, the duality ingrained in my blood, and how the fierce independence of the West and the deeply rooted tradition of the East shaped me. My culture is one of oppositions, of a constant balancing act between tradition and progress, between holding on and letting go. It is a duality that has often left me feeling torn between two worlds, between the person I was and the person I was becoming.

In many ways, it mirrors the contradictions of the industry I have devoted myself to—the world of hospitality, where luxury and chaos coexist, where precision and spontaneity walk hand in hand. It is in this delicate balance, this dance between what is and what could be, that I have learned to find myself. Not as a finished product but as a work in progress.

I look now at the present moment, having spent nearly two years at the Iconic Hotel before stepping into the next phase of my journey at another new hotel. These two months offered me the space to reflect, to rediscover the spark of passion I thought I lost. Here, under the guidance of Barb, I am once again growing—reawakening my joy for this work, rekindling my passion for hotel management, and learning that perfection was never the goal.

I celebrate my imperfections, the small victories each day, and the people in my circle who continue to shape me. Even in the moments of doubt, I find humor and connection, and it is these simple joys that anchor me. Even so, this moment, as freeing as it may be, did not come without its price.

My older son and I remain estranged, a painful wound that lingers, unanswered and unresolved. The ache of that loss follows me.

My younger son, still with me, fills my days with meaning and a desire to be the best mother I can. Through it all, my mother stands by my side—her unwavering belief in me, her love and encouragement have been the constants in a world that has never quite stopped shifting.

Despite this, even as I find new joy in my work, I know there are shadows that linger—the echoes of mistakes, the heartbreaks I have yet to mend. There are days when the burden of the past feels overwhelming. Still, I am learning to carry it. I am learning to dance through it. In this moment, as I look back on the years, I realize how much of my journey has been about finding peace with the unknown. Finding meaning in the spaces where I thought there was none. Coming to terms with the fact that there will always be more to discover, more to learn, and more to become. This has led me to accept that there is no perfect time to become whole. There is only the process of discovery and the understanding that we are always, always becoming.

I recall Dostoevsky's musings on the human condition, his ability to delve deep into the cracks of the soul and pull out the most enlightening truths. In his words, I find a resonance with my own journey. "Man is what he makes of himself," he writes in *The Brothers Karamazov*. I would argue that she is also what life makes of her, what the world does to her, and how she responds to it.

The process of self-forging, shaped by the raw material of experience, is neither clean nor simple. It is a jagged path, full of twists and turns, and sometimes it feels like it would be easier to let go—to stop striving. I have come to understand that it is that very struggle, that search for meaning, that defines us. Thus, as I reflect on the path that has brought me here—back to a place where I can find meaning in my work, in my life—I understand now that the true journey is not about reaching some end, some final destination. It is about finding joy in the steps along the way, in the broken pieces, and in the quiet realization that we are all, at our core, a work in progress.

That, perhaps, is enough.

CHAPTER 30

The Power of Self-Compassion

I realize that the most penetrating lessons that shaped me have not come from the moments when I felt invincible but from those when I crumbled under the weight of my own expectations. These vulnerable snapshots, when the world demanded everything from me and I no longer performed or pretended, led me to learn a lesson I had always struggled to understand: the power of self-compassion.

Growing up in a Russian household, strength was not optional. It was expected. Emotions, especially vulnerability, were weaknesses. My culture, deeply rooted in stoic resolve, taught me that to show discomfort, to express pain, or to ask for help were signs of failure. We didn't cry in public. We didn't ask for support. It was an ideal both deeply ingrained and stifling, shaping the way I viewed myself and the world around me.

I carried this belief with me into my career. For much of my early adult life, I pushed through pain, ignored exhaustion, and refused to acknowledge cracks forming beneath the surface. I held the belief that displaying vulnerability would be a sign of weakness, and that I needed to project an image of strength and stability, regardless of internal turmoil. This belief became my armor, my way of protecting myself from the world's judgment. That said, it was also my undoing.

There came a point when the weight of this self-imposed strength became too much to bear. My life, both personally and professionally, reached a critical juncture. I could no longer hold everything together. I reached my limits, and I was forced to confront something long avoided: that real strength lies not in the ability to withstand everything without faltering, but in the ability to soften, to accept our flaws, and to embrace our vulnerability.

It was during these difficult moments I learned what true strength meant. It wasn't about perfection, performance, or the absence of weakness. True strength, I learned, is the ability to extend compassion to oneself. It's accepting the messiness of life without judgment, recognizing that we don't have to be flawless to be worthy of adoration, respect, and understanding.

It was not an easy realization to come to. At first, the idea of showing myself kindness felt unnatural. It was foreign to me, like a concept I couldn't fully trust. As time passed, I recognized that to move forward, I had to start where I was—broken, imperfect, and human—and show myself the same kindness I so often extended to others. In the depths of those years, I found myself withering beneath the weight of my own expectations. I thought I could push through the pain and pretend that everything was fine—that I was fine. I had convinced myself that if I kept going—if I kept moving forward with determination and grit—the broken parts would eventually fall into place—but they didn't. Instead, they became more fractured, more hidden. The more I tried to keep it together, the more I lost touch with who I was. It wasn't until I understood that healing did not require me to be whole again, but to accept that I had never truly been whole to begin with.

The truth I had been avoiding was simple, yet thought-provoking: I wasn't perfect, and I didn't have to be. This was the beginning of a slow unraveling—one that would lead me not to the abyss I feared, but to a different clarity. It was not the kind of clarity that comes from fixing things—from achieving or succeeding—but the kind that comes from surrendering to the reality of my own humanity.

I encountered the concept of *Kintsugi*, the Japanese art of repairing broken pottery with gold, and it resonated with me in ways I couldn't fully articulate at first.

In Kintsugi, the cracks in a piece of broken pottery are not hidden or disguised. Instead, they are filled with gold, celebrated as part of the item's history and beauty. The brokenness doesn't diminish the object; rather, it enhances its uniqueness, turning it into something even more precious.

This philosophy became my own. For much of my life, I viewed my flaws and vulnerabilities as something to hide— something to be ashamed of. In time, through Kintsugi, I saw that those cracks— moments of pain, imperfection, and vulnerability—could be what made me whole, what made me beautiful in my unique way. The shatteredness wasn't something to be erased but something to be embraced. Like the pottery, my cracks became part of my story, and they were made beautiful with the right care.

I started to see my life in a new light. Instead of trying to erase the broken parts of me, I learned to acknowledge them, to fill them with compassion, understanding, and love. I recognized that I was not defined by my cracks but by how I chose to respond to them. It was through this act of self-compassion that I began to rebuild, not to become "perfect," but to become whole in a new, more insuppressible way. It took years for me to accept this. I spent years masking my pain, running from my vulnerability, and trying to prove to both the world and myself that I was worthy.

At some point, however, I had no choice but to stop. To stop running. Stop pretending. Stop the exhausting charade. I had no choice but to face the fractured version of myself that I had been desperately trying to avoid. In that confrontation, I realized healing did not require me to be whole again, but to accept that I had never truly been whole to begin with. It was this acceptance—this radical self-compassion—that became the foundation for my healing.

I also found support in my tribe, the people who held space for me during my darkest hours. They showed me that vulnerability wasn't a weakness but a gateway to deeper connection. Through them, I understood that strength was not shown by standing alone but through leaning on others when needed, being open to receiving love and care when I had nothing left to give. I realized that self-compassion was not a luxury—something reserved for the weak or the self-indulgent. I had been taught to believe that compassion, whether toward others or myself, was something that would undermine my strength, my resolve.

However, as I understood what self-compassion truly meant, not coddling myself or avoiding hard truths; it acknowledged my pain and my flaws with kindness, treated myself as I would treat a dear friend, with tenderness and patience. Self-compassion let go of the unrealistic expectations that shaped my sense of self-worth and allowed me to simply be—flawed, messy, and imperfect.

It wasn't only my relationships that taught me about self-compassion. It was the small, personal practices I adopted to reconnect with myself. I recorded my dance videos—something simple, but deeply liberating. In those moments, I allowed myself to experience joy, feel free, and be fully present without judgement. I remember as if it recently happened—the day I recorded my first video. It was set to a song that evoked feelings of heartbreak and anger. Despite that, as the months went by and I continued recording, I chose more and more positive songs. Dancing became my way of finding light in the darkness, a reminder that even in painful times, there was space for joy.

Through the wisdom I found in books and teachings, I also learned to embrace the impermanence of life. Authors like Brené Brown, Mel Robbins, Beth Kempton, and Oliver Burkeman taught me valuable lessons on vulnerability, courage, and the fleeting nature of time. In particular, the philosophy of *Wabi-Sabi* and the teachings of Kintsugi helped me to understand that imperfection and impermanence are not things to be feared but to be embraced.

There is beauty in the cracks, in the fleeting moments of life, and in accepting that nothing lasts forever. Consequently, I approached my work with a new mindset. This world, which had always mirrored my own evolution, became a place where I rediscovered my passion. I remembered why I loved this work in the first place: the ability to create moments of connection, to serve others with kindness, and to be a source of light in a world that often felt dark.

I also learned to appreciate small victories. I celebrated moments when I showed up for myself, even when it was hard. I realized I didn't have to have everything figured out. I didn't have to be perfect. I needed to show up with compassion, be willing to ask for help, and relish the process, flaws and all.

This practice of self-compassion has been one of the most transformative lessons of my life. It has taught me that true strength doesn't lie in avoiding pain or perfection but in allowing ourselves to feel it, learn from it, and then move forward with grace. Thus, perhaps most importantly, I am learning to love myself—not in spite of my flaws, but because of them. This is because, similar to Kintsugi, the light shines through the cracks. It is in those cracks we find the true beauty of our human experience.

As I continue this journey of self-discovery, I carry with me this lesson: that I am worthy of compassion, I am worthy of love, and I am worthy of embracing my imperfections as part of what makes me whole. This journey is not one toward becoming perfect but embraces becoming more fully myself—broken, mended, and always growing.

CHAPTER 31

Hospitality as a Way of Life—Purpose

Healing, growth, and self-discovery rarely reveal themselves as clean and straightforward paths. They emerge, instead, as tangled knots—woven of triumphs and failures, mistakes and insights, moments of clarity buried deep within layers of confusion. My journey, similar to the lives of numerous individuals I've observed in the hospitality industry, has not been a linear path. It has been a series of fragmented, sometimes disorienting, moments each an essential piece of a greater, ever-evolving picture.

The transformation I sought—one full of clarity, of knowing exactly who I was and where I was going—was not something that arrived in a single, dramatic revelation. Rather, it crept into my life as a quiet, steady unfolding. In the beginning, I imagined that growth would come in grand, thunderous waves—shifting the very ground beneath my feet. Yet, as I have learned, it is not the moments of loud, sweeping change that shape us the most. It is the subtle, imperceptible ones—the fleeting conversations with a team member that went beyond task lists and toward the heart; the awkward, sometimes humbling attempts at new hobbies that taught me to relinquish control; the quiet, unsung beauty in the imperfect moments where everything fell apart, yet something extraordinary emerged. These moments taught me the most, these fragments reshaped my perspective on leadership, service, and ultimately, my very self.

Countless times I looked for external validation, believing that the only way forward was through grand gestures or visible triumphs. Yet the true transformation in my life came not from these outward achievements but from the invisible shifts within—the self-compassion, when I allowed myself to be vulnerable, to acknowledge my flaws without judgment, and to rest in the knowledge I didn't have to be perfect.

I remember, too, the slow yet steady lessons I absorbed as if they were etched into me with each passing day, in the kitchens, the meeting rooms, and behind the scenes of the hospitality world. These were not lessons of polished techniques or strategies; they were lessons in being. Being present. Being human. Being real.

I didn't fully comprehend the essence of hospitality until I immersed myself in its core. The work itself, in its purest form, is about meeting people in their most authentic state—offering them space to be who they are, with all their messiness and imperfection. Understand that leadership, in the truest sense, is not a position of power but a commitment to service—an ongoing, evolving process of showing up for others with deep empathy, humility, and a willingness to share in their struggles and triumphs.

I've often heard people speak of leadership as though it were something to achieve—a status to be earned or maintained. What I've come to grasp is that leadership is a constant practice, not a static achievement. True leadership, I have discerned, is not about knowing the answers or having a clear vision at all times. It requires courage to be present, vulnerable, and giving. It's willingness to guide by example, not to dictate, but to walk beside those led, and in doing so, create an environment where others feel empowered to reconcile their own imperfections.

The industry itself, this world of hospitality, has been my greatest teacher. It is in this environment, rife with challenges and moments of grace, that I understood the complexities of leadership and personal growth. The lines between the two blurred, and I saw that lesson one was inseparable from lesson two. My personal growth mirrored the growth of my leadership. The more I allowed myself to embrace the discomfort of vulnerability, the more I saw the same transformation take place in those I worked with. It is in those quiet segments of empathy, of shared understanding, that the deepest connections are made, and the greatest growth occurs—not only professionally, but personally. There were times I questioned my place in this industry, wondering whether I was cut out for the demands. Yet over time, I came to understand that the essence of hospitality is in presence. It takes courage to show up, be human, and give without expectation. This became my guiding light in times of doubt—a light that flickered but never fully went out, even in the most challenging of times.

As my journey continued, I found myself not only growing in my role as a leader but also as a mentor. There is a delicate beauty in mentorship—something that requires not only giving, but also listening, learning, and sharing in the vulnerabilities of those you guide. Mentorship imparts knowledge, yes, but it also offers the wisdom of experience and creates a safe space for others to learn, to stumble, and to rise again. In this way, I came to realize that leadership is not a solitary pursuit. It is a collective act, rooted in compassion, connection, and a shared commitment to growth.

Through the years, as my understanding of leadership deepened, so, too, did my understanding of purpose. I no longer saw hotel management simply as a job or a career. I came to see it as a calling—a way of life that mirrored my evolution. It was not about success, recognition, or accolades. It was about the quiet, consistent act of serving others with authenticity, with heart, and with the knowledge that in doing so, I was also serving myself.

In each guest interaction, in each moment of connection, I found not only purpose but a deeper understanding of what it means to be truly alive. In this work, I discovered the fundamental truth that purpose is not something we find in grand gestures or moments of recognition. In the everyday choices we make—showing up for others, leading with empathy, and accepting human imperfections—we find it. My purpose, I came to see, is rooted in the simple, small acts of service, connection, and understanding. Amid these moments, the light that once seemed so distant shone brighter—gentle, steady, and always present.

Looking back, I see my journey has been much more than a professional path. It has been a spiritual quest—a process of becoming whole, of embracing my humanity, and of learning to serve others in a way that reflects the deepest values of compassion, empathy, and care. Along the way through this process, I unearthed that leadership is about embracing imperfection, learning from mistakes, and always striving to serve with a full heart. The journey continues.

Each day, each interaction, each moment of vulnerability brings new lessons, new opportunities for growth, but I am no longer searching for dramatic revelation. The deepest truths are not hidden in extraordinary moments but in the ordinary ones—the quiet acts of connection, the humble service, the moments when we show up for each other with compassion, respect, and a willingness to revel in the beauty of being human.

As I continued my journey in hospitality, the lessons I learned on leadership—empathy, vulnerability, presence—also guided me toward a deeper understanding of myself. I realized that true growth, both as a leader and as a person, lies not merely in serving others but in finding joy and connection in the simple, everyday moments that keep us grounded and whole.

CHAPTER 32

Embracing Joy and Presence in the Everyday

In reflecting on my journey, I realize that the most transformative moments haven't come from grand breakthroughs but rather from the subtle shifts that happen quietly, over time. It wasn't always the monumental events that shaped me, but the small, unnoticed instances that gradually led to deeper understanding. These moments, often tucked away in the folds of the everyday, are the ones that have helped me reconnect with myself in more clarifying and meaningful ways. The process of growth, I've learned, doesn't always scream for attention. Sometimes, it hums in the background of our lives, inviting us to notice the details, to savor the simplicity, and to find joy in the mundane. It's in these simple instances—whether it's laughing at our own imperfections or sharing small, unspoken connections—that I've discovered the depth of transformation. These are the moments I want to hold onto as I continue my journey.

The Power of Small Practices. Transformation doesn't always need to be grand. In fact, it's often found in the smallest of moments—like the time I decided to attend hip-hop dance classes with two of my closest friends. It wasn't about becoming a dancer or perfecting the moves. It was about doing something together that allowed us to laugh at ourselves, especially when we found ourselves out of sync with the melody.

In front of that mirror, all of us struggling to follow the instructor, I felt a sense of freedom. We weren't trying to impress anyone. We were simply laughing at the awkwardness of the moment, enjoying each other's company and the music. It was in that laughter that I discovered joy—not as a performance or goal to reach but as something that can live in the process itself, in the imperfection.

I also found bliss in smaller, quieter moments—like having a chocolate chip cookie every morning for breakfast. Yes, it wasn't the healthiest choice, but it was my small indulgence. Additionally, beyond the sugar rush, it gave me an excuse to connect with my pastry team, to share in those fleeting moments of camaraderie and lightness. Every bite, every exchange of jokes over a tray of cookies, reminded me that connection often happens in the most unexpected places. In that moment, the cookie wasn't only a treat—it was a bridge, a way for me to feel rooted in something small but meaningful.

Embrace moments of spontaneity, like trying new food spots around town. Whether it was an authentic El Salvadorian restaurant with flavors that immediately transported me to a different culture or a new gelato shop that became my guilty pleasure, these small adventures brought me joy in the simplest of ways. It wasn't the food—it was being present in my surroundings, immersing myself in the industry I treasure as a consumer, and witnessing the authenticity of each experience. From the way the flavors told a story to the way the food was served with pride, each moment deepened my connection to the world around me.

Connection: Strength Through Vulnerability. The more I leaned into these small practices, the more I understood the importance of connection—not only to myself but to others. Healing doesn't happen in solitude, and growth doesn't emerge from monumental experiences. Sometimes, it's the quiet, shared moments with those around you that truly make the difference. Like my pastry team, my friends from that dance class, or the people I met on my food adventures—each connection, no matter how brief, was a reminder that we're not meant to do this alone. In the laughter shared with my friends in that dance studio, I realized how powerful vulnerability can be. We weren't afraid to be silly, to mess up, to not look perfect—and in doing so, we created space for something more beautiful than perfection: genuine connection. It's these moments that hold true strength, the kind that isn't built from standing firm and unyielding, but from allowing yourself to lean into vulnerability, to be seen for who you truly are, and to see others in return.

The Beauty of Imperfection: Filling My Cracks with Compassion. I'm still on this journey of self-discovery, and I continue to find that healing doesn't come from fixing every flaw. It comes by accepting them. The cracks are where the light can get in, where the grandness of life's experience can shine through. Whether it's accepting the imperfections in my dance moves, savoring an indulgent cookie, or relishing the authentic simplicity of a meal shared with a stranger, I've come to see that imperfection is not something to be ashamed of, but something to be celebrated.

There are still days when I struggle with this. I want to be flawless, to fix all the things I see as weaknesses. However, the more I practice showing myself kindness in the face of imperfection, the more I realize that these cracks aren't something to erase—they're something to honor. They're the moments that make us who we are, and they can be the source of our greatest strengths.

I remember looking at an old photo of myself—one from a time when I felt broken, like I had no direction. In that photo, I saw the sadness in my eyes, but I also saw a strength I didn't recognize at the time. The cracks were always there, but they didn't define me. They were simply a part of the journey, and now, I embrace them with compassion.

Practical Tools for the Journey. This journey of self-discovery isn't something you can complete in a day, a month, or even a year.

It's ongoing. Though along the way, I've found that small practices, if done consistently, can support us as we move forward. These tools have helped me through challenging times, and they might offer something meaningful for you, too, wherever you are on your own path.

Moving Forward with Presence. I am still on this journey. I am still learning and growing. What's more, I'm learning that healing doesn't have an end point. It's about being present with where I am right now. It's showing up for the moments, however small they seem, and finding meaning in the everyday practices that connect me to myself and others. This is a journey without a destination. It's ongoing, and that's okay.

The small acts of presence—whether it's dancing, laughing, connecting with others, or simply being kind to myself—are the practices that keep me moving forward. These practices will continue to support me—and perhaps you—as we walk the path of self-discovery together.

As I reflect on all I've learned, I realize that the real beauty of this journey lies not in the grand moments or the milestones, but in the quiet spaces between them—the intervals that often go unnoticed. It's in the stillness of a breath, the warmth of a simple gesture, and the quiet strength that emerges when we allow ourselves to be vulnerable, to be seen, and to be human. I carry these lessons with me, with a heart full of gratitude—for the people, the experiences, the challenges, and the joys that shaped me.

Albeit I also carry a sense of peace because I now know that it's okay to not have all the answers. It's okay to be unfinished—to be in process. There's a quiet wisdom in that uncertainty. It's where the true growth happens—not in the perfection of who we are, but in the grace we extend to ourselves as we unfold, day by day.

So, I move forward—no longer searching for a perfect version of myself, but embracing the ever-evolving, ever-changing nature of who

I am. I cherish the contradictions, the messiness, and the beauty in the imperfections. I move forward with presence, with love, and with a deep trust that, as the moments that shaped me have led me here, they will continue to lead me toward new lessons, new experiences, and a deeper connection to the world and to others. For this is not the end of the journey—it's simply the beginning of a new chapter. I embrace each new chapter with an open heart, confident that I am precisely where I am meant to be.

CHAPTER 33

Final Reflections:
The Legacy of Hospitality

There comes a moment in every journey when we look back and realize that the path we have walked was not simply taking us to a destination but holding us while we become someone new along the way. For me, hospitality has always been more than the skillful delivery of services or the technical proficiency of a particular industry. It has been a force of transformation, shaping not only my career but also my way of moving through the world.

I think back to my grandmother's kitchen, where my understanding first took root—not in spoken lessons, but in the silent language of care, in the way she prepared a table, in the way she gave of herself so effortlessly. At the time, I did not yet know that these small, intimate moments would lay the foundation for my entire philosophy on life and leadership. That said, the echoes of those early lessons have followed me through every phase of my professional and personal evolution.

Through the years, I have learned that hospitality is not confined to restaurants, hotels, or dining tables. It is an extension of human connection, a bridge between cultures, a language spoken in gestures rather than words. I have seen it in the unrestrained joy of an Indian wedding procession, in the disciplined elegance of high tea service, and in the warmth of a shared meal where no one is a stranger. I have felt it in a genuine smile from a host, a quiet reassurance from a leader, an unspoken understanding between two people who may never cross paths again but, for a fleeting instant, belong to the same story.

Hospitality makes space for others—not simply in the physical sense, but in the emotional and spiritual sense as well. It sees people—truly sees them—and acknowledges their worth through action. It gives the grace of generosity, the humility of service, and the power of creating experiences that linger far beyond the moment.

Now, as I reflect on this journey, I see how every experience—every hardship, every triumph, every lesson—has not only shaped my understanding of hospitality but also my understanding of myself. It is no longer simply an industry or a skill; it is the lens through which I view the world. It is the legacy I hope to leave behind, not only in the spaces I have worked but in the lives I have touched. If there is one truth I have come to understand, it is this: hospitality is not something we do—it is something we are. It is the way we move through life, the way we choose to treat others, the way we create meaning in the smallest of gestures. It is an art, a philosophy, and a calling.

Ultimately, perhaps it is also the most human thing of all—the desire to welcome, to nourish, to connect, and to belong. I have seen this truth reflected back to me in the most unexpected ways. When I hear stories of success from people whose lives I have touched, when I witness the seamless ballet of a perfect service, when I see my team working together to create something unforgettable—I know, deep within me, that I have had a hand in something greater than myself. When I look at my son, at the way he moves through the world with authenticity and kindness, I recognize that the values I have spent a lifetime cultivating have taken root in the next generation. My Russian soul feels full when I see people smiling, immersed in the moment, lost in the beauty of shared experience. Then, there are quiet moments.

Standing by the water as the sun sets, I feel the weight of the day lift, knowing that no matter how small, I made a difference today.

This business is not about grandeur, it is about significance. It is about leaving the world, or even a single moment, better than we found it. Thus, to those who read this, I offer this call to action: Find your own way to revere hospitality.

Whether in leadership, in daily life, or in the simple act of being present for another human being—choose to welcome, to uplift, to create something meaningful. Recognize that hospitality is not focused on serving but on seeing. Understanding that, regardless of where we come from, we all seek the same thing: to be acknowledged, to be received with open hands, to belong.

Hospitality is evolving. More than ever, I see people passionate about service, elevating experiences beyond expectation. Nevertheless, I also see the creeping influence of transactionality, the slow shift away from genuine care toward efficiency. This is where we must stand firm. The soul of hospitality management is not in systems or strategies but in people—in the way we make others feel seen, valued, and cared for.

So I ask you—whether you are in this industry or simply navigating the world as a human being—to be stewards of hospitality's legacy. Protect its heart. Let your presence be an invitation, your service an act of generosity, and your leadership a testament to what it truly means to care. Because no matter how much the world changes, one truth remains: "I've learned that people will forget what you said, people will forget what you did, but people will never forget how you made them feel" (Maya Angelou).

As this chapter closes, the journey does not end. The work of hospitality, like life itself, is never truly finished. It is an ongoing conversation, an evolving practice, a continuous act of creation. So, I move forward, not with a conclusion, but with an open door—ready to welcome whatever comes next.

Acknowledgements

"To serve is not to disappear—it is to become."
— *A New Life, A New Menu*

Writing this book was a return—a pilgrimage through kitchens and corridors, through memory and migration, to the tables where I first learned that service could be sacred.

To my sons: You are my breath and ballast. You are why I continue. Through your eyes, I rediscover joy, truth, and the possibility of becoming anew. You are my living legacy.

To my mother and grandmother: Yours were the hands that taught me to feed with purpose, to love in silence, to endure without recognition. This book was grown from the seeds you planted.

To my family, by blood and by choice—across oceans, across seasons, across generations: Thank you for carrying me when I could not walk on my own.

To those who appear in these pages by name, my "tribe": Thank you for shaping my story. Whether our time was brief or boundless, your presence mattered. Your impact lingers.

To the many I met along the journey—cooks and servers, housekeepers and dishwashers, leaders and guests: You are the soul of this story. Though unnamed, you are everywhere in these pages, in the rhythm, in breath, in the heartbeat of each chapter.

To Cortni Merritt, MA: Thank you for your editorial clarity, your soulful care, and your gift for hearing what lives between the lines. You helped this book speak in its truest voice.

And to you, the reader: Thank you for taking a seat at my table. May these words feed something brave and tender in you. May you remember:

Your story is sacred. Your presence, enough.

You belong.

Author Bio

Marina Baronas is a hospitality executive, mentor, and storyteller with over twenty-seven years of leadership experience in food and beverage operations across the United States and Europe. Born in Germany and raised amid the cultural layers of Lithuania, Russia, and Azerbaijan, she immigrated to the United States in search of belonging—not as destination, but as practice.

Now based in Tampa Bay, Florida, Marina draws from her lived experience as an immigrant, a mother, and a leader to inspire others to lead with empathy, reverence, and presence.

Her debut memoir, *A New Life, A New Menu: An Almanac of Belonging*, is a lyrical meditation on food, exile, identity, and the invisible hands of service. Rooted in kitchens and dining rooms both remembered and real, her writing reflects a deep commitment to emotional truth, cultural memory, and the quiet, enduring strength of women who serve without applause.

Whether guiding future leaders or steeping tea at her kitchen table, Marina believes that hospitality is not a profession—it is a philosophy and a form of love.

MARINA BARONAS

• NEW LIFE, A NEW MENU •

• NEW LIFE, A NEW MENU •

• NEW LIFE, A NEW MENU •

www.ingramcontent.com/pod-product-compliance
Lightning Source LLC
Chambersburg PA
CBHW042029050526
44107CB00104B/851